Pilgrim Guide To Scotland

Pilgrim Guide To Scotland

Donald Smith

SAINT ANDREW PRESS
EDINBURGH

First published in 2015 by
SAINT ANDREW PRESS
121 George Street
Edinburgh EH2 4YN

ISBN 978-0-86153-862-1

British Library Cataloguing in Publication Data
A catalogue record for this book is available from the British Library.

It is the publisher's policy to only use papers that are natural and
recyclable and that have been manufactured from timber grown in
renewable, properly managed forests. All of the manufacturing processes of the papers are expected to conform to the environmental
regulations of the country of origin.

Typeset by Manila Typesetting
Printed and bound in the United Kingdom by
CPI Group (UK) Ltd.

In Memoriam
Andy Hunter
1954 to 2015
True Pilgrim

Be thou a bright flame before me
Be thou a guiding star above me
Be thou a smooth path below me
Be thou a kindly shepherd behind me
Today, tonight and for ever.
(*Ascribed to St Columba*)

Pilgrim Guide to Scotland
Pilgrim Routes

Table of Contents

Route Four – Perthshire Circles: The St Fillan and St Serf Pilgrim Journey   81

Route Five – Coming to the Clyde: The St Mungo Pilgrim Journey   95

Route Thirteen – By Northern Coasts: The St Maelrubha Pilgrim Journey   223

Route Fourteen – On the Sea Roads: The St Magnus Pilgrim Journey   243

Acknowledgements

In pursuing local pilgrimage I have consulted innumerable local guide books and histories, and more recent websites. I have explored the locations, discovering that many standard guides are not always accurate primary sources, often repeating other guidebooks.

A notable exception to this is Nigel Tranter's *Queen's Guides to Scotland*, which are exemplary in their local knowledge, though unfortunately not covering the whole of Scotland. Among older books James Rankin's *A Handbook of The Church of Scotland* is a treasury of information about medieval parishes, dioceses and dedications. Finlay MacLeod's recent pocket-sized guide *The Chapels of the Western Isles* is a model of clarity and on-the-ground knowledge.

Edwin Sprott Towill's alphabetical *Saints of Scotland* remains a useful reference book, though modern scholarship has in some respects overtaken it, not least with Alan MacQuarrie's landmark edition of *The Aberdeen Breviary*, which was originally commissioned by the great Bishop William

Elphinstone of Aberdeen as one of the first printed books in Scotland. How extraordinary that it should take five hundred years to reprint the Breviary with an English translation and commentary – published by Four Courts Press in Dublin. Also from Ireland's Four Courts Press comes Pádraig Ó Riain's magisterial *A Dictionary of Irish Saints*, which is full of information relevant to Scotland.

The prayers and reflections, including the Psalms, are my own new translations from original sources, or my adaptations from traditional materials ranging from early Celtic nature poetry to Alexander Carmichael's *Carmina Gaedelica*. I gratefully acknowledge permission to quote from Nan Shepherd's *The Living Mountain*, re-published by Canongate Press in *The Grampian Quartet*. I also acknowledge my own earlier brief introduction to this topic *Celtic Travellers: Scotland in the Age of the Saints*, which was published by The Stationery Office to mark the 1400th anniversary of St Columba in 1997. The prayers and reflections are only ascribed where there is one known specific source or author.

Finally, I have to thank my wife, Alison, and my children who sometimes found themselves, when young, trudging gamely through some unlikely looking places in pursuit of a goal visible mainly to my inner eye.

I dedicate *Pilgrim Guide to Scotland* to Ann Davies, Brian Fraser, John Hume and Stuart Brown who in different ways have been true champions of Scotland's Pilgrim Journeys. They are excellent friends on the journey, and unfailing wells of enthusiasm, commitment and knowledge.

Saint Andrew Press gratefully acknowledges the support of Scotland's Churches Trust and The Drummond Trust, Stirling.

Pilgrim Guide to Scotland

Introduction

The first human beings were nomads, so journeying is part of our earliest consciousness – fundamental to our cultural genetics. Pilgrimage adds a spiritual underlay to the journey without losing any of the other sensations or experiences of travel. Traditional pilgrimages remain vital to expressing religious faith in many cultures worldwide, including in Europe. But more recently, in the developed world, there has been a renaissance of pilgrimage. In this sense a modern pilgrim travels open to new reflections and insights without necessarily subscribing to a specific faith, tradition or belief.

Scotland is exceptionally well placed to offer traditional and contemporary pilgrim journeys. The terrain is varied and expansive, austere and beautiful by turns. Our landscapes and townscapes are imbued with millennia of spiritual awareness from megalithic stone circles to beehive Celtic cells, monasteries, cathedrals, and today's churches, mosques and temples. Our history is a vivid tapestry of human achievement, vanity and folly.

There is a diverse abundance of journeys and destinations available in Scotland, from busy centres to isolated places of peaceful contemplation. The fourteen Pilgrim Journeys offered in the guide are a rich and wide-ranging geographical selection, yet not exhaustive. Furthermore, many different forms of travel are available, by sea and land, though all should involve, even if in imagination from an armchair or sickbed, a sense of walking. Rhythmic footfall renews a connection between our modern consciousness and that ancient sense of mother earth and the cosmos, without which we are strangers of a passing moment.

Rhythm is an important part of pilgrimage – day and night, departing and arriving, marking the morning, midday and evening stages. This Pilgrim Guide provides these patterns for each day and journey, while also offering themes and reflections appropriate to the different locations. Those who wish to find out more about a particular place or stage can get further details on travel options and places of interest in each area on www.scotlandspilgrimjourneys.co.uk and www.scotlandschurchestrust.co.uk. Visitors and explorers can also research local information and accommodation on www.visitscotland.com, and through web searches by locality. Online and paper maps are part of the fun and essential requirements on the way. Remember that in many mountainous or remote parts of Scotland mobile phone networks may not always be available.

The Pilgrim Journeys set out in the Guide can be completed as a whole, or experienced in parts over weeks, months or even years. The time taken on any complete or part of a journey will vary depending on your modes of travel. Each stage of the journey has its own coherence, but you may choose to branch off to a nearby place of interest or combine parts of different journeys, according to choice and convenience. Always be prepared to follow your instincts or curiosity, and depart from the plan! This book has emerged from a lifetime of exactly such open exploring in many parts of Scotland, sampling the diverse ways in which places and people can be encountered in our many-splendored big, wee country.

In that light, I would like to outline some perspective on the religious meaning of pilgrimage, while recognising that the motives for going on such a journey vary widely. As already described, contemporary pilgrims may simply be travellers open to a different dimension, but for some travellers there may be a specific reason arising from bereavement or another life crisis, including mental or physical illness. For others the impulse may be a nagging sense of something missing; or an aspect of life left unexplored and fallow; or a desire to experience our spiritual heritage at first hand.

The twenty-first century is sceptical of God and other concepts of the divine. Yet early Celtic saints and mystics were also aware of the absence of God, alongside their vivid sense of God's presence in the physical universe. Contemporary pilgrimage recognises that God is hidden, while being open to some unexpected intimation or spiritual presence. In Scotland the landscape is often veiled in cloud or mist, when an unpredictable shift in the atmosphere can light up the whole outlook.

The steady rhythm or pattern of pilgrimage accepts that God is not obvious, literal or predictable. We have to be disciplined and peaceful, while open to the unexpected. Pilgrimage nurtures an openness to the divine in everything. Light is everywhere, unseen yet also the means by which all things are perceived in their true shape and colour. Underlying, background awareness may gently intrude, while in some instants the invisible impinges with penetrating brightness, bringing joy or sometimes sadness, because of our awareness of the vulnerability and transience of life.

Few people are now convinced by a pat religious scheme in which all our troubles are attributed to humanity's 'original sin', which can in turn be cancelled out by Christ dying on a cross. Would this not be a strange way for a loving God to behave, and anyway how can it account for underserved suffering in the human and natural worlds? Does God need to be justified to humanity in such a fashion, or humanity justified to God given that, in this faith tradition, Christ unites the two?

Our experience of pain, oppression and injustice cannot be explained away; most of the genuine religious visionaries regard it as a troubling mystery that carries us to the paradoxical heart of what it means to be human. Without suffering we could not experience the compassion and love which are the highest values of conscious life. Pilgrimage travels with mystery, journeying through our mixed experience, while enabling some measure of acceptance, insight, consolation and perhaps renovation. We cannot at a stroke shake off our personal or collective burdens, but we can lighten the load, or just see things in a new light. The Christian invitation is to journey in faith, hope and love.

Finally, it is worth noting that contemporary pilgrimage in Scotland is reconnecting with older cultural layers and traditions that were lost through socio-economic change, including migration and clearance. Moreover, pilgrimage was often actively discouraged or suppressed after the Scottish Reformation. Many special sites were neglected and forgotten. But Scotland has five millennia of continuous cultural evolution already behind it, and that carrying stream continues even if its flow is sometimes underground, biding its time to break out afresh. Of course things are reinterpreted and changed by new generations, yet going on pilgrimage in Scotland today we discover that angels and ancestors still keep their ancient places.

I myself have found great satisfaction, and joy, in exploring these older traditions with contemporary eyes. If this guide provides some companionship on the road then it will have fulfilled its modest purpose.

Donald Smith

Historical Note

When Was Scotland?

The political entity which we now call Scotland did not emerge until the ninth century. Before that, there were four main cultural groupings each of which maintained its independence. These were the British of southern Scotland, the Picts who occupied the northern mainland and most of the islands, the Scots of Dalriada in Argyll who were closely linked with northern Ireland, and the Anglo-Saxons of Northumbria whose territory had expanded to the River Forth.

From 800 CE a fifth group, the Norse peoples of Norway and Denmark, raided and then settled large parts of northern Scotland including the Western and Northern Isles.

Of these five groups three – the Picts, the Scots and the British – were Celtic peoples, though belonging to different branches of the Celtic language tree. The Norse and the Saxons were also linguistically and culturally related, but nonetheless bitter rivals for land and power. In most of the areas they conquered, a sub-stratum of Celtic people continued to exist and in due course to mix with the invaders turned settlers.

Ironically, the Viking incursions of the ninth century were a major catalyst towards the foundation of a single Scottish kingdom. First the Picts and Scots united under one royal dynasty (though not without continuing coups and feuds) and then the British kingdom of Strathclyde was annexed. By this time the steady spread of Christianity had become a significant common factor in the cultural make-up of the diverse yet related peoples of northern Britain. In due course the Norse also adopted the religion, whose treasure they had once aggressively plundered.

Who Were The Saints?

The early saints were Scotland's first missionary travellers, and the direct successors of the apostles who were instructed by Jesus to live a life of poverty, teaching and healing 'on the road'.

More specifically, in Scotland the early saints flourished between the foundation of Whithorn in Galloway sometime after 400 CE and the sack of Iona by the Vikings around 800 CE. The successors of the early saints were the Culdees, 'servants and companions of God', who continued the Celtic traditions of the early saints until the reigns of Queen Margaret and her pious descendants, which

stretched from 1066 until 1296, laying the foundations of a close relationship between the Scottish
Kingdom and medieval Christendom that was to
last until the Scottish reformation in 1560.

While respecting the spirituality of the native
Church, Queen, later Saint, Margaret paved the way
for the continental monastic orders and the parish
system to be established in Scotland. Nonetheless,
the heritage of the early saints remained influential,
providing a mosaic of local traditions and cultural
patterns that endure to this day. Most people know
the 'big names' such as Columba or Ninian, but every
area has its local associations and dedications which
constitute an intricate spiritual geography closely
linked with the natural environment and Scotland's
cultural diversity. The term 'Celtic Christianity' has
sometimes been used to describe this, but it is a mis-
leading later invention that obscures rather than illu-
minates the multi-coloured and multi-cultural ways
in which early Christianity evolved in Scotland.

When Was Protestant?

Protestantism came to Scotland in an official Calvinist
form in 1560, after earlier Lutheran influences were
suppressed by Scottish monarchs allied with Roman
Catholic France. The consequences were deeply political, leading to civil war and, in due course, to the
Union of the English and Scottish Crowns under
James VI and I in 1603.

Roman Catholicism survived in a few parts of Scotland in an underground way, while over the next two hundred years competing Protestant ideas of church governance and of its role in the state battled it out in often violent conflict. Not until the nineteenth century did religious tolerance enable different Christian traditions to develop alongside the legally established Kirk, which continued in its Presbyterian and Calvinist form while still subject to internal divisions and secessions.

Pilgrimage and traditions of the saints were early victims of the new Calvinist order, discouraged and then actively suppressed as 'heathen', 'papist' or both. The nineteenth century saw the first stirrings of revival led by Roman Catholic and Episcopalian perspectives, but in the twentieth century most Christian denominations were recovering some sense of pilgrim journeying, often in ecumenical forms.

However, as demonstrated by this book, the official organs of church and state were never wholly effective in eradicating local customs and beliefs. In many areas of the country people preserved local connections and stories, and continued to hold certain places and seasons as sacred. Though religion needs its reformers there is also wisdom in continuity. In older Highland culture it was the custom to 'smoor' the fire at night, covering it over with turf so that the embers could be uncovered in the morning and stirred back to life.

STARTING OUT ON A FIRST MORNING

Ask the loveliness of the earth
                Of the sea
                Of the wide airy spaces
                Of the sky.

Ask the pattern of the stars,
the sun making lights with its rays,
the moon softening the darkness of the night
that follows.

Ask living things that move in the waters
which linger on land
which soar through the air,
ask the souls that are hidden
and the bodies that feel and see,
visible things that must be steered,
invisible things that guide –

Ask all these things, and they will answer,
'Look, see, we are lovely.'
Their loveliness is their confession.
And these lovely but ever changing things,
who has made them, except beauty
unchanging?
(*St Augustine*)

BLESSING

May the road rise up to meet you,
May the wind be always at your back,
May the sun shine warm upon your face,
And the rains fall soft upon your fields.
And until we meet again,
May God hold you in the palm of his hand.

Route One
Source South-West:
The St Ninian
Pilgrim Journey

Whithorn in Galloway is the cradle of Scottish Christianity. Yet it is also a place of mystery, since we know very little about St Ninian or Nynia. It has even been suggested that Ninian is actually St Finian of Ireland and, though this is speculation, there was certainly early and very close connection between Whithorn and the Irish Celtic Church. Later, Whithorn was also linked with the Northumbrian Church.

The area is exceptionally rich in accomplished early Christian carvings, which are displayed at Whithorn. The later Priory was, moreover, a wealthy centre of medieval and royal pilgrimage. Yet what impresses today is the remote simplicity and austere beauty of the place. Most pilgrims in past times went there by sea from England and Ireland as well as Scotland, and the shoreline chapels and retreats are an integral part of the Whithorn experience.

We offer two routes to Whithorn. One is a cross-country journey through Scotland's borderlands into Galloway. Royal penitents such as James IV traversed this way. There is also a western way by Glasgow and the Ayrshire Pilgrim Trail, connecting the abbeys, cathedrals, palaces and castles of Scotland's kings. You may choose to make a circuit going by one route and returning by the other.

Whatever your approach, the destination is a world apart, unobtrusive yet evocative of a spiritual otherness that is so rare in contemporary life.

MORNING

The heavens declare the glory of God;
And the firmament shows forth his making.
Day unto day utters speech;
And night unto night shows knowledge.
There is no speech or language;
And their voice is not heard.
But their sound has gone out through all the earth;
And their words to the end of the world.
In the heavens he has pitched a tent for the sun
Who comes out like a bridegroom,
A champion who delights to run the race.
It rises at one end of heaven
And runs a circuit to the other
And nothing is hidden from its warmth.
(*from Psalm 19*)

BLESSING

Following the rivers
Walking ancient paths,
Kentigern our guide,
Ninian our destination,
Glimmer of hidden light
On sacred ground.
May peace be in our steps
Meditation in our rest
As all creation
Breathes the mystery.

Stage 1: Edinburgh to Abington

Travelling south from Edinburgh you enter the borderlands of British Celtic Christianity, which gave birth to Ninian. Influenced by Rome and the eastern Mediterranean Church, missionary Saints such as Ninian, Kentigern or Mungo, and later Cuthbert, bridged cultures to root the new faith in traditional soil.

A first diversion takes you to Rosslyn Chapel where European Christianity meets Celtic traditions in a cornucopia of sacred legend, inspired by medieval tradition, not Dan Brown's entertaining *The Da Vinci Code*. In Penicuik, the ancient church dedication is to St Mungo or Kentigern, while its site by the Esk is a clue to the origin of the town's name – 'Hill of the Cuckoos'. Continuing south, you enter the Lyne and then the Tweed valley where, at Stobo Kirk with its ancient chapel, you touch the same world of early faith. Here also the legends of Arthur took root and further up the valley, at Drumelzier, Merlin was reputedly baptised by Mungo before undergoing a threefold mystical death experience. A stone and 'burial' mound mark the traditional sites by the river.

Turning back out of the Tweed valley you come to Broughton with its ancient church of St Llolan on the hillside at the northern end of the village, before crossing to Biggar and then south by Lamington into the Clyde Valley. Here you intersect again with St Mungo's missionary way, and its pilgrim station by the Clyde at the ruined chapel of St Constantine, a British Celtic King to whom the great monastery at Govan was dedicated. A later King Constantine was slain by the Vikings at Fife Ness, adding to the holiness of his name and lineage.

Stage 2: Abington to Newton Stewart

Crossing the hills into Dumfries and Galloway you traverse another frontier. The landscape is different here, with hilly terrain and river systems pointing to the Solway. The cross-country way is testing whatever your means of travel, but the villages with their handsome churches provide stopping places and their own rewards. This peaceful beauty belies an earlier history of proud Gallovidian independence clashing with Irish invaders, Scottish Kings, Saxon expansion from Northumbria, Norse settlers and English invaders. Yet to this day the forests, hills and valleys retain a sense of stubborn resistance and integrity. Only the hardy warrior, the courageous missionary, or the truly penitent could maintain the necessary determination to reach their goal.

By Thornhill, Penpont, Kirkland, Moniaive, St John's Town of Dalry, New Galloway, and Minnigaff, you arrive at Newton Stewart, gateway to the Machars of Galloway. Surprisingly few people traverse this secluded and very characterful part of Scotland, which is rich in history and religious traditions, from medieval parishes to hardy

religious dissenters such as the seventeenth-century
Covenanters.

Stage 3: Newton Stewart to Whithorn
By Wigtown

Crossing the River Cree into the Machars you begin
to feel pilgrim routes converging. Old pilgrim bridges
with historic churches mark the closer stages. Wigtown
is the former county town with its inheritance of persecution and martyrdom in Covenanting times, and
its modern booktown status.

From here you sense the sea, and the contours low-
ering towards coast and dune. Whithorn itself misleads with its sleepy market town air till, approaching
the priory with its associated heritage centres, you
begin to experience the extent and depth of its history. Even here, though, there is more underground
than is visible, as successive religious communities,
British, Irish and Scots, constructed a cluster of
shrines and pilgrim sanctuaries. From the humble
beginnings of a whitewashed Candida Casa dedicated to St Martin of Gaul, Ninian's missionary community grew in sacred stature far beyond its original
humble situation. The prestige of Scotland's Christian
birthplace was cultivated by later Kings and Bishops.

But Whithorn is also a gateway, the focal point
of a sacred radius that includes the dramatic Cave
or Refuge of Ninian on the shore, and the moving
arrival point and chapel at Isle of Whithorn. The

whole quiet peninsula is redolent of the original humility, remoteness and spiritual intimations which brought Ninian here in the beginning. Underlying all is the distinctive wheel cross, carved and illustrated throughout the area. Combining sun and sacrifice, creation and salvation, the wheel cross is an enduring symbol of the missionary Christianity which fashioned a new faith in ancient patterns.

Views from the Machars include the Isle of Man and Ireland with all their linking seaways. On the west side are the open waters of Luce Bay, looking across to the Mull of Galloway. Here by Glasserton and Port William you connect with the other major route into Whithorn. Our description will also return you here via the great western pilgrim route.

ON THE WAY

The stories about Ninian reflect a kindly, practical person, which is why he is often portrayed as the first Bishop, a father of pastors and shepherds.

SAINT NINIAN AND THE LEEKS

Now it so happened one day that the blessed Ninian came into the refectory to share a meal with the brothers. When he saw that there were no vegetables or herbs laid out on the table, he called for the brother who was responsible for the community's garden.

'Why are there no leeks or herbs laid out for the brothers today?' Ninian asked.

'In fact, Father', the gardener replied, 'I dug up the earth today and planted out all the seedlings I had left, but the ground has not yet grown anything worth eating'.

'Go and gather whatever you can find to hand and bring it to me', instructed Ninian gently. The brother was amazed and not a little alarmed. He was unsure how to act. Nonetheless he went slowly out to the garden. An astounding sight met the worried gardener's eyes. Those very seeds and seedlings he had planted that morning had grown to full vigour, even producing their own seeds. The poor man was gobsmacked, as if in a daze or trance. He thought he was seeing a vision. But then, all things are credible and possible to those who have faith.

At last he regained his senses and, recalling the power of the saintly Abbot, the gardener gave thanks to God, picked the vegetables and, returning to the refectory, placed them in front of Ninian. All present were delighted, exchanging glances, and praising God with heart and mind. God who works wonders through his saints and servants. Finally they departed with minds and souls better fed than their bodies had been on the luscious green leeks.

NINIAN'S STAFF

Many stories were told about the things Ninian had done to help the people of Galloway. People said that he had been a holy man with special powers and that even his staff had been able to work wonders.

According to one story, a teenager had run away from Ninian's school at Whithorn. He knew that he would get in trouble because he had skipped school and gone drinking in the village. So when he ran away he took Bishop Ninian's staff with him, since he believed it had special powers.

Anyway, the lad ran down to the shore looking for a boat in which to escape because Whithorn is by the sea. Sure enough, there was a currach on the beach.

Now a currach is a little boat made of supple branches bent together to make a frame. Over the frame are stretched some hides or animal skins, and then oil or grease is rubbed in to make them waterproof. Only two or three people can fit in a small currach.

So the boy jumped in and put to sea. The only problem was he hadn't noticed that the currach had the normal frame of twigs or branches, but no skins. Immediately water flowed into the boat. All thought of running away disappeared. But could the boy be saved from drowning?

No problem: the boy laid Bishop Ninian's staff against the waves, and water stopped filling the boat. Then he held Bishop Ninian's staff up like a mast with a sail and the currach began to skim over the water. Finally, he put Bishop Ninian's staff into the sea over the back of the currach, and it acted like a rudder, steering him safely back to the shore.

You can be sure he wasn't in a hurry to run away again. As for Abbot Ninian, he was more amused than angry, but he tried not to show it.

People said that if Ninian's staff was stuck in the ground, the dry wood would put out roots, draw sap, shoot out branches and leaves, and produce flowers and fruit.

Then at the foot of the tree a pure crystal stream would well up, full of sweet-tasting, life-giving water. Well, after all, Ninian was a very holy person!

BLESSING

May the Lord of Hosts
Be your guard and guide
In high hills and green pastures
By river banks and forest paths.
A staff to comfort,
His presence to shield,
And at every stage
The blessing of strangers,
The pilgrim's welcome,
And a table laid.

Stage 4: Edinburgh to Glasgow
By Linlithgow and Stirling

Follow the pride and glory of the Stewart Kings from their capital city of Edinburgh with its Palace, Abbey and Royal Castle, to the great chateau at Linlithgow by the lake. Here also is the medieval Church of St Michael towering above the burgh town. Continuing to Stirling you encounter another Royal Castle and Palace with its attendant Kirk of the Holy Rude and ancient burgh. The worldly power and devoted piety of the Kings and Queens of Scots appear as two sides of the same coin, till all was submerged in bloody civil war and religious conflict between Protestant and Catholic, leading first to Union with the English crown and subsequently the Westminster Parliament. But the wars of Church and State continued into modern times with Covenanters, Royalists and Parliamentarians struggling to assert the relative authorities of kirk, crown and parliament, in Scotland, England and Ireland.

Leaving Stirling you reconnect with the missionary saints. At St Ninian's the historic church is probably a foundation of Ninian himself. Note the freestanding traditional tower, probably replacing a Celtic round tower. From here the followers of Ninian moved north into Pictish territory, carrying the Christian message into the Grampians. Our route, though, heads south-west by the Carron Valley, Kilsyth and Kirkintilloch. It was also travelled by the early Celtic missionaries with the line of the hills on the north hand and the Antonine Wall on the other. Approaching from the north side you realise why Glasgow was known as 'a dear green place' sloping to the River Clyde, with its back to the sheltering hills.

St Mungo came by the Antonine Wall route, and founded his settlement on the site of what is now Glasgow's medieval Cathedral. It breathes a truly spiritual glory, expressed in superb medieval architecture and modern stained glass. The tomb of Mungo can still be visited in its crypt beneath the original high altar.

'May Glasgow flourish by the preaching of His word and the praising of His name' is the city's motto, and few places can claim so many fine churches, including the now restored St Mary's Roman Catholic Cathedral by the river, St Mary's Episcopal Cathedral and St Luke's Greek Orthodox Cathedral in the West End. Downriver at Govan the 'People's Cathedral' – Govan Old – still sits within a Celtic monastic enclosure rich in early carved stones.

Stage 5: Glasgow to Kilwinning
By Paisley

Travelling downriver on the south side of the Clyde, Govan Old Church is on the near side, while on the north side Dumbarton Rock, citadel of Strathclyde's ancient Celtic kingdom, rises above the river. Pressing on, you turn into Paisley with its 'holy hill' of churches and, in the town below, the medieval Abbey. Established by St Mirren, this religious community flourished under the patronage of the royal Stewarts and remains a centre of devotion, and a jewel in the crown of Paisley's rich cultural heritage. St Mirren's Roman Catholic Cathedral is the mother church of the Paisley Diocese.

Continuing through Renfrewshire by scenic Lochwinnoch, and the historic churches of Beith and Kilbirnie, you cross into Ayrshire. At Kilwinning Abbey the medieval foundation is home to a later parish kirk. This is the gateway to North Ayrshire with easy access to Largs, and then the Cumbrae Islands, or to Ardrossan and Arran. In Millport on the Cumbraes, the Cathedral of the Isles is an astonishing nineteenth century revival church, and a focus of modern retreat.

Arran offers a circuit of ancient places of worship, many associated with St Molaise. He was an important Irish saint connected with St Columba and with St Blane of Bute. An old pilgrim walking route connects his burial place at the cemetery above Shiskine with his retreat or refuge on Holy Island in Lamlash Bay. Pilgrims came here from Ireland crossing on the last stage from Saddell Abbey in Kintyre. Holy Island is now a Buddhist retreat centre.

Hear the call of the West
Following river and coast
Till the shape of the land
And the sight of the sand

Guide our weary souls
By sea, island shores
To green peace and rest.

Stage 6: Kilwinning to Maybole and Crossraguel

Going south through central Ayrshire you come by Prestwick to the county town and port of Ayr itself. The many churches here represent both the history and also the culture that shaped Robert Burns, who is much in evidence. By way of his birthplace at Alloway, you continue close to the coast through beautiful countryside and historic villages to Maybole, bearing in mind his great anthem to humanity, 'A Man's a Man'.

Then let us pray that come it may
As come it will for a' that,
That sense and worth o'er a' the earth
May bear the gree for a' that
For a' that an a' that
It's comin yet for a' that
That man to man the warld o'er
Shall brithers be for a' that.

Burns is a product of the enlightened, liberal Protestantism espoused by his father, but opposed by Presbyterian traditionalists of the kind satirized in 'Holy Willie's Prayer'. At the same time, nurtured from his mother's knee by the folksongs and stories of Ayrshire, Burns sows the seeds of the Romantic movement. All of his work is infused with religious and moral principles, that spill over into Burn's radical politics.

Just south of Maybole are the impressive ruins of Crossraguel Abbey, a Cluniac monastery and important centre of Ayrshire's culture in medieval times. The history here is marred by religious and clan conflict, not least the notorious torture of the last Abbot by the Earl of Casillis, determined to seize the Abbey's lands. But these former conflicts cannot outweigh the dignity of these well interpreted remains. They tell a story of pilgrimage in former times and remind us of old traditions now renewed.

Stage 7: Crossraguel to Glenluce
By Stranraer and the Mull of Galloway

As the crow flies the direct way to Whithorn is from Girvan by Glentrool Forest to Newton Stewart, a wild and secluded route to this day. But there is more evidence of pilgrims keeping by the coast to experience the churches and the hospitable inns by the sea.

Stranraer is not only a departure point for Ireland but gateway to the Rhinns of Galloway. This peninsula has its own fragile aura, bathed in eastern light and replete with early Christian sites, carved stones and sanctuaries. A circuit, taking in the Mull, has the feel of an island, ringed by more than thirty churches and ancient chapels, many of them barely visible. St Medana or Triduana is supposed to have fled here from Ireland to escape a suitor. When he pursued his quarry to the Rhinns, she offered him her own much-admired eyes on a skewer. She is also remembered at Restalrig in Edinburgh with a notable healing well for eye diseases, and at Westray in Orkney, suggesting an even remoter refuge.

In addition to the Whithorn influence, the Rhinns are close to Ireland and a natural stopping place on the western seaways between Wales, the Isle of Man, Ireland and the Hebrides. Among many evocative sites are the carved stones at Kirkmadrine, the medieval Church of Kirkmaiden with the nearby cave and chapel of St Medana, Chapel Patrick at Portpatrick, St Mary's at Kilmorie and St Columba's Chapel at Kirkcolm. In addition to the present day churches, Soulseat Abbey on the neck of the peninsular is a reminder of the remarkable religious heritage of this small yet special area.

St Mary, St Patrick, St Bride, St Medana,
St Cuthbert, St Donnan, St Finian, St Columba,
St Catherine, St Ninian, St Molaise, St John,
Go with you.

East of the Rhinns is Glenluce Abbey which is the gathering point for the approach to Whithorn. Walkers can still arrive here from the standing stones at Laggangairn with their pilgrim crosses, and the nearby chapel and Wells of the Rees at Kilgallioch. On gentler contours continue into the Machars by Chapel Finian (an arrival point for seaborne pilgrims) to Whithorn.

Stage 8: Glenluce to Whithorn

Whithorn itself misleads with its sleepy market town air, till approaching the priory with its associated heritage centres, you begin to experience the extent and depth of its history. Even here, though, there is more underground than is visible, as successive religious communities, British, Irish, Northumbrians and Scots, constructed a cluster of shrines and pilgrim sanctuaries. From the humble beginnings of a whitewashed Candida Casa dedicated to St Martin of Gaul, Ninian's missionary community grew in sacred stature far beyond its original humble situation. The prestige of Scotland's Christian birthplace was cultivated by later Kings and Bishops.

But Whithorn is also a gateway, the focal point of a sacred radius that includes the dramatic Cave or Refuge of Ninian, and the moving arrival point and chapel at Isle of Whithorn. The whole quiet peninsula is redolent of the original humility, remoteness and spiritual intimations which brought Ninian here in the beginning. Underlying all is the distinctive wheel cross, carved and illustrated throughout the area. Combining sun and sacrifice, creation and salvation, the wheel cross is an enduring symbol of the missionary Christianity which fashioned a new faith in ancient patterns.

Views from the Machars include the Isle of Man and Ireland with all their linking seaways. On the west side the open waters of Luce Bay, looking across to the Mull of Galloway. Here by Glasserton and Port William you connect with the other major route into Whithorn.

EVENING

God bless this house from roof to floor,
And the door, God bless us all for evermore.
God bless this house with fire and light;
God bless each room with thy might;
God with thy hand keep us right;
God with us dwelling through this night.

BLESSING

White shining house,
Candida Casa of Martin,
Ninian's home of wonder,
You are our witness.
Guide of all pilgrims,
Be destination and departure
Our homecoming harbour

And our slipway.
Take us to the seashore,
Be a rock fast refuge
And grant safe passage
On our ocean voyage,
Now and for evermore.

Route Two
Further from Ireland:
The St Columba
Pilgrim Journey

Columba's epic journeys by sea and land form the cultural and sacred geography of Scotland. Dramatic scenery unveils a story of exile, penitence and peace. Key sites on this route can also be explored in Scottish Gaelic – Slighe Chaluim Cille – and Irish – Sli Cholmcille – on www.colmcille.org.

The range of these journeys is enormous, from Donegal through Kintyre and Argyll, to Iona, and then through the Great Glen to Inverness and on to Tain and Portmahomack. The Argyll side of the journey also contains many island-hopping options in the Inner Hebrides.

Though the reasons remain unclear, Columba took the path of exile in 563, arriving eventually at Iona, where he founded his main religious community in Scotland. From there he and his followers radiated out across the Highlands and the Islands leaving few places untouched by his influence. Though many other missionary Saints from Ireland were involved in this movement, such as Moluag, Maelrubha, Cainnech and Donnan, it is Columba's story that has become identified more than any other with the marriage between Celtic culture and early Christianity, and between Scotland and Ireland.

Tradition has it that Columba only returned once in his life to Ireland, to settle affairs between the Kings of Ireland and of Dalriada in Argyll, and to save the poets of Ireland from banishment. We are fortunate in still possessing some of Columba's own poems, along with many more composed in a Columban tradition. In addition Adomnan's 'Life of

Columba', dating from around 800 CE, is a master-work of early Scottish literature.

Yet what connects most with us across the centuries is the sense of a restless, visionary personality, powerfully influencing all around, journeying on yet ever seeking inner peace – his own place of resurrection.

MORNING

Columba. Dove.
Dove of the Church
Royal Prince of Ulster
Chaluim Cille of the Battles
Toast of Poets, Scriber of Psalms
He takes the Sea Road
Green Martyrdom of Exile,
He sails for Alba.

BLESSING

Bless to me,
The waves beneath my oars,
The stars by which I steer,
The earth beneath my feet,
The path on which I tread.
Bless to me,
That on which my mind is set,
That on which my love is set,
That on which my hope is set,
The way on which I go.

Stage 1: Inveraray to Campbeltown

Loch Lomondside forms the eastern flank of Argyll and has its own missionary patron, Saint Kessog. By Luss, Tarbet and Arrochar, you approach the mighty guardian of Argyll, Ben Arthur or The Cobbler. The Rest and be Thankful pass then crosses to Loch Fyne and to Inveraray, seat of the Dukes of Argyll and chiefs of mighty Clan Campbell. This beautiful little town by the shining loch is a perfect starting point for pilgrimage.

Going south to Lochgilphead and then Tarbert, on your left hand Loch Fyne opens into the Firth of Clyde, affording magnificent views at each stopping point. Tarbert itself is the ferry point for east Argyll and Cowal. At Skipness Castle, with its ruined chapel of St Brendan, you look over to Arran and to Bute, the beautiful sanctuary island of St Blane. Continuing by the fishing village of Carradale, you reach Saddell where Somerled, Lord of the Isles, founded a Cistercian Abbey, and is buried. This was the departure point for medieval pilgrimage to the mountainous island of Arran whose dramatic peaks dominate the skyline. It is still a place of peaceful contemplation. The pilgrimage crossed to the burial place of St Molaise and then over to that saint's rocky hermitage on Holy Island.

Finally near the southern end of the peninsula you reach handsome Campbeltown, capital of Kintyre. You are now very close to Ireland and to Columba's first point of arrival, though the older name of this settlement, Kilkerran, suggests that the church here had its own missionary founder – St Ciaran.

Stage 2: Campbeltown to Tarbert, Loch Fyne with Islay and Jura

Leaving Campbeltown, we continue south on the coast round the bay, by the old church of Kilkerran. Davaar Island, another place of Celtic retreat, is in the bay. Traditionally Columba's first landfall in Scotland was near the Mull of Kintyre, where Southend and St Columba's Chapel at Keill are now located, looking out to Sanda.

It was no use though, since Ireland is still close and clearly visible. This was not sufficient as an exile, or perhaps Columba could not trust himself to stay away from his homeland in Donegal and his community in the oak grove by the Foyle, that we now call Derry/Londonderry.

So the weary voyagers put back to sea, and we resume our journey following them north, by Glenbarr and Killean. At Tayinloan you can take a ferry to Gigha – God's Island – which is dedicated to Blane's uncle, St Catan. The route then continues by Clachan to Tarbert. Tarbert is the departure point for Islay and Jura, if desired, and the gateway back into mid Argyll.

The southern Hebrides are imbued with Columba's spiritual influence. On Colonsay Columba founded a daughter community from Iona, having perhaps made another landing place at Oronsay at the southern end, from where Ireland was still visible. Mountainous Jura, with the Corryvreckan whirlpool at its northern end, is a likely location for Columba's special retreat, while Islay's spacious landscape was later home to successive Lords of the Isles, principal patrons of Iona and the medieval Church in western Scotland.

To understand these connections you need good sea legs as well as a map. The ferries from Tarbert go to Port Ellen in southern Islay and Port Askaig on the east. From Port Askaig you can make the short hop to Jura or continue to Colonsay. Both routes, in Columba's time, could be sea roads north to Iona. Columba's principal settlement was not remote but a crossroads. This was its making as a centre of the Celtic world, and later its undoing when Norse raiders arrived on the same sea routes.

By land on Islay, you can circuit from Port Ellen by the Kildalton Cross. This classic work of Celtic art portrays David's combat with a lion, the spilling of Abel's blood, the offering of Isaac and, at the centre, Mary and the Christ child surrounded by angels, all encompassed by the circle of creation. Continue then by Bowmore, Portnahaven, Kilchiaran, Kilchoman, Kilnave, and Finlaggan to Port Askaig. These names with their associated churches, ruined chapels and carved crosses, breathe a rich Christian heritage.

On Jura there is just one principal road north. If Columba's retreat was here it would have been at the rocky north end looking onto Corryvreckan, which is recognised to this day as a remarkable place of natural power and cosmic energy.

Stage 3: Tarbert to Lochgilphead and Crinan

From Tarbert the route north, by the west side, follows a loop round wooded Knapdale, looking onto Loch Tarbert and then the Sound of Jura. There are good views of Gigha, Islay and Jura from this coast road. Swinging north to Kilberry you reach the centre of scenic Knapdale with Kilberry Castle and St Brendan's Chapel, housing their fine collection of medieval carvings.

Continuing north you reach Achahoish, where the present parish church of South Knapdale is sited. However, west of the village, near Lochhead farm, there is an old burial enclosure and above it Caisteal Tor, where the Dun or fortress of King Conall of Dalriada was located. He was Columba's cousin and tradition has it that Columba came here seeking Conall's help. So the exile was directed towards Iona. In commemoration of this, further round the loch, is St Columba's Cave screened by an attendant ruined chapel. The cave is undoubtedly an ancient place of sanctity testifying to the Columba tradition, and pilgrim offerings are left on the altar shelf.

Though walkers may continue on this route to the Point of Knap, road vehicles must return east across

Knapdale to Inverneil, and then come west again via
Lochgilphead. Back on the west side, two long points
reach south on the respective shores of Loch Sween.
On the east you arrive at the forbidding Highland
fortress of Castle Sween and the church of Kilmory
Knap with its carved crosses. On the west lies
Tayvallich and then Keills Chapel with another set of
outstanding carvings in its shelter. But both routes,
though rewarding, are time consuming, because the
only way back is to retrace your steps. An easier
option is to go straight on to the attractive canal village of Crinan. It was all much simpler for Columba
in his boat, slipping in and out of these sea lochs!

Stage 4: Crinan to Oban

From Crinan you turn north into an area of Argyll
whose concentration of sacred sites is unrivalled
except perhaps in Orkney. On the left hand is the
citadel of Dunadd, where kings were inaugurated,
and on the right Kilmichael Glassary with its ancient
dedications to St Michael and St Bride. Columba
participated in the inauguration at Dunadd of Aedan,
Dalriada's most famous ruler.

Next comes Kilmartin Glen with its complex of
cairns and standing stones; then Kilmartin with its
carvings, church and museum. Above Kilmartin lies
Carnasserie Castle where John Carswell, the first
Protestant Bishop of Argyll and the Isles, translated
John Knox's liturgy into Gaelic.

Whatever the twists and turns of historical circumstance, the overwhelming impression is of an all-embracing sacred landscape, which may be pointing us further north. Each year brings new discoveries and a deepening sense of the many generations who have left their markers here for us to contemplate and ponder.

A roll-call of beauty and historical interest lies ahead with the villages of mid-Argyll from Ardfern and Craignish to Kilmelford and Kilninver. A detour to the inner islands of Seil and Luing reminds us that the sea is ever present. Rocky Scarba looks onto the Corryvreckan whirlpool, while on the Garvellachs the beehive cells of the early contemplatives still stand. Both can only be reached by small boat. The association here is with St Brendan rather than Columba, but there is a common desire – the hunger for solitude on the edge of the ocean.

Stage 5: Oban to Iona

The ferry crossing to Mull from Oban skirts the north end of Kerrera, and then the southern end of Lismore. The story is that the followers of Moluag and of Columba raced to see who could touch the great sanctuary island first. Columba's boat was a length ahead when Moluag cut off his finger and threw it ahead onto the shore, so winning the contest. Unlikely history, but Lismore did become Moluag's headquarters, reminding us that Columba was not alone in his mission to Scotland.

The Ross of Mull has a distinctive character and community which is not simply a road to Iona, and Mull itself deserves wider exploration on the return journey. The history of the Ross is closely linked with the story of the people of this area which can be explored in Bunessan, on the island church, and in the Iona Heritage Centre.

Iona itself is Columba's Isle, though it was a sacred place before he arrived. The restored Benedictine Abbey should be experienced as part of the whole island with its many places of peace and beauty, including the ruined nunnery and the ancient burial ground of Scotland's kings at St Oran's Chapel. Martyr's Bay, where Viking raiders slaughtered the later monks, and Columba's Bay, which was the Saint's own landfall, are all evocative of the island's special atmosphere and story.

The restoration first of the Abbey Church, and then, through the leadership of the twentieth-century Iona Community, of the Abbey buildings, is one of Scottish Christianity's resurrection stories that continues to resonate internationally. Again Gaelic tradition, of which Columba himself was such a notable champion, foresaw this development:

Iona of my heart, Iona of my love,
Instead of monks' voices will be the lowing of cattle;
But ere the world will come to an end
Iona shall be as it was.

ON THE WAY

Happy for me to be on an island
In the breast of the sea
On a rocky pinnacle scanning the ocean
Watching its glittering waves
As they chant a melody to the Father
Of the world's turning course.
Happy for me to see a level sparkling strand
And to hear the song of the birds
Music of happiness to hear the sound
Of the crowding breaking waves upon the
headland
Crying beside the rocky church
And splendid flocks of birds
On the ocean face and the mighty whale
Heaving wonder of the sea
In its ebb and flood –
O that my secret name should be,
He who turned his back on Ireland.
(*ascribed to St Columba*)

COLUMBA AND THE CRANE

One night, on Iona, the monks were settling
down to sleep. It was a stormy night and black
clouds were scudding by with fierce gusts of
wind.
'Go down to the shore and keep watch',
Columba said to a young monk, 'because

we're expecting a visitor.' The young monk was amazed. 'But, father', he said (the monks have always called their abbot or leader 'father') 'it's a wild night. No-one could possibly cross over to Iona tonight. They'd drown in the storm.' Columba just looked, and the boy knew there was no use in arguing. When a holy person like Columba took a notion there was no putting him off.

The young monk went down to the bay where the boats landed. Hugging his robe around him, he paced up and down, trying to keep warm. No boat appeared. He was getting really wet and was just about to give up when he saw something against the edge of a cloud.

At first it was just a black blur or smudge, but as it got nearer he realised it was a bird flying towards the island. Then the monk saw that it was a crane beating its wings against the wind, and it was losing height. The crane's long neck stretched out towards the land, but it was weakening in the gale.

Lower and lower the poor exhausted bird came, lost, far from home, its wings encrusted with sea salt, till down it came at the edge of the surf. The boy rushed forward and, catching up the great bird in his arms, he brought it to land, wrapped it in his robe, and carried the soaked and quivering bundle back to the monastery. 'Good', said Columba. 'I see that you have found our visitor.'

For two days the boy looked after the exhausted bird. He laid it by the kitchen fire and fed it drops of warm milk and little pellets of bread. 'Take good care of him', said Columba, 'for that crane was nested where you and I were brought up, in Ireland.'

After two days the storm had cleared and the crane was stronger and restless. So, binding up the bird once again in his robe, the young monk carried it to the shore.

There he cast it free and with a strong, steady beating of its wings the crane rose into the open sky, its long neck pointing across the sea to Ireland.

BLESSING

As we move through this place of light
our darkness is illumined, and our burdens laid down.
Here the veils are thin, boundaries transparent.
We are passing through, yet for a moment,
time is suspended.

Stage 6: Iona to Mallaig

Iona became a destination for Columba, but it was also the staging post for wide-ranging journeys that radiated across the Highlands and Islands of

Scotland, or Alba as it was then known. The next stage of our journey is equally expansive, passing through the wide spaces of Mull, and crossing by ferry into the sparsely inhabited region of Morvern. In Columba's time these were the borderlands between the Kingdom of Dalriada with its Irish ties, and the Pictish peoples of the mainland.

At Salen on Loch Sunart, there is a choice between continuing west into Ardnamurchan or turning immediately north into Moidart. The rough lands of Ardnamurchan were heavily wooded in Columba's day, and the monks of Iona came often by sea, fishing and foresting. They treated Ardnamurchan as if it were another island, but nowadays there is a significant trail by road to the dramatic Ardnamurchan Lighthouse which is the westernmost point on the British mainland. There is a fine St Columba's Well at Ardslignish on the south side, with magnificent views over the lochs. St Catan was buried at Columba's instigation in the lovely little Bay of the Strangers below. There is a very old church at the end of a narrow road on the north side at Kilmory, and another, the Church of St Congan, at Kilchoan on the south.

Moidart, leading into Arisaig and Morar, offers gentler pastures with ancient woods reaching to the lochs and silver sands. The area has a strong religious heritage reaching through Columban and medieval times to the Jacobite era, when Moidart remained loyal to the exiled Stuart kings and their Roman Catholic faith. At Eilean Fhinnin by Dalilea there is St Finnan's Church with its ancient bell, and the burial ground of the Clanranald Chiefs. In 1745 Bonnie Prince Charlie left here to raise his standard at Glenfinnan, but in 1746 he left here again permanently for Europe after his defeat at Culloden. The road ends at Mallaig though the sea roads continue from there to Skye, the small isles of Canna, Rum, Muck and Eigg, and to the Outer Hebrides. All of these are Columban journeys as the personal influence and heritage of the Saint spread. At this juncture however our route continues by land.

Stage 7: Mallaig to Spean Bridge/ Inverroy

Returning through lovely Arisaig we follow the route towards Fort William by way of Glenfinnan where Bonnie Prince Charlie first raised his standard. Coming to the junction of Loch Eil and Loch Lochy at Corpach, we are able to visit busy Fort William. However this later garrison and port town screens the earlier castle and settlement of Inverlochy. The entrance is signed on the left of the A82 coming out of Fort William. The Castle is an intimidating Highland fortress on the mouth of the River Lochy, flanked by its old church and burial ground. It is along the banks of the Lochy that Columba, like so many travellers and armies since, came on his epic journey to Inverness and beyond.

The modern road takes us on the line of the later military road to Spean Bridge. The original church settlement here was at Kilmonivaig down towards the Lochy. Leaving the main road east towards Roybridge, we move into the heartlands of the Keppoch MacDonalds. Arriving at the chapel and burial ground of Cille Choire (key on post at cottage at foot of access road) we are raised above the valley with spectacular views across Lochaber. This is clan and Highland country as it was before militarisation and modernisation. These are the wild lands that Columba set out to traverse with his few companions.

Yet Columba's journey planted a lasting legacy. In modern times the family of Mary McKillop, the pioneering Australian educationist and missionary, emigrated from here. Her recent canonisation is proudly celebrated in the local churches. At Cille Choire the spiritual heritage of centuries is palpable, the peace still physically present. There is a monument close to the church to Iain Lóm MacDonald, Gaeldom's finest seventeenth-century bard.

Stage 8: Roybridge to Inverness

Going back to the Great Glen we follow the journey undertaken by Columba with his fellow Saints, Cainnech or Kenneth, and Cormac. They both had Pictish connections, which was useful as the expedition went deeper into unknown territory.

Just short of what we now know as Fort Augustus, the locals warned them of a water dragon blocking their passage across the river. But Columba sent one of his monks to swim the crossing and when the monster appeared he banished it to the depths of Loch Ness where it still resides. The settlement here came to be called Kilcumin after one of Columba's successors as Abbot of Iona. St Cumin's church was sited in a bend of the River Tarf where the ancient burial enclosure can still be seen. Fort Augustus came later, as did the Benedictine Abbey, which occupied the site of the former military garrison until it was united with Pluscarden in Moray.

Undeterred, the Columban party pressed on. At Invermoriston just over the modern bridge, Columba purified a well which the locals told him was cursed. The well is still there – Fuaran Chaluim Cille – and though the church Columba founded has gone, the burial ground can still be seen, guarded by standing stones.

At Inverness the cluster of Pictish fortifications shows how important this location had become. Here was the centre of northern Pictish power. The tradition has Columba confronting it head on, possibly at the capital of the High King Brude on Craig Phadraig. After commanding the gates to swing open, Columba challenged the Chief Druid by demanding the release of an Irish slave girl. Whether converted or just canny, Brude made his peace with the fiery Saint, and Columba was allowed to found a church on the riverside site of what is now the High

Kirk. Inverness is full of fine churches including the Episcopal Cathedral of St Andrew across the Ness.

Stage 9: Inverness to Portmahomack and Tain

For many centuries we presumed that Inverness was the end of Columba's pioneering road. But then modern archaeology uncovered a Columban monastery on the north end of the Nigg peninsula at Portmahomack. The situation is perfect, above a gentle beach and landfall, with monumental views along the Moray Firth and north into Sutherland. Here, truly, Columba saw Alba in all its beauty and epic expanse.

Did Columba find a place of resurrection, a place of peace, in this special location, after all his labours? Visit the baptismal pool, and the excellent museum in Tarbat Old Church but, most of all, stand on the gentle slopes where Columba stood, look and ponder. For a time perhaps, there was peace, but then the Saint had to return to Iona where he was eventually laid to rest. But long afterwards his remains came west again into the heartlands of Alba.

The Portmahomack Monastery is strategically sited. It is a vital staging post on the sea road of the Saints, which carried Columban missionaries round the north coast of Scotland and then south by Aberdeenshire, Angus, Fife and Lothian, all the way to Lindisfarne in Northumberland. The journey here from Inverness comes by way of a string of religious sites at Beauly, Fortrose, Cromarty, Nigg and Fearn Abbey. Just to the west is Tain, the famous medieval burgh and royal pilgrimage centre dedicated to St Duthac. A little further north you quickly reach Dornoch, with its rugged Cathedral, missionary gateway to Sutherland and Caithness.

EVENING

Helper of those who labour,
Ruler of all good,
Defender of the faithful,
Who lifts up the humble
And puts down the proud.
Judge of all judges,
Pure life of the living,
Shining light of hope,
We implore, being low and frail,
Trembling and wretched,
That you draw us on
Through the unending storm of life
To the beautiful lofty haven
Heaven, infinite home
Of Christ our King.
(*St Columba*)

BLESSING

To you before the end of day
Creator of the world we pray:
In love unfailing hear our prayer,
Enfold us in your watchful care.

Route Three
Dee, Don, and Spey:
A Grampian Saints'
Pilgrim Journey

The popular surviving image of pilgrimage in Scotland looks to the west with Iona and Whithorn. But much of the energy of the early saints, including the Irish voyagers, was directed east. It is not hard to see why since the great land mass of Scotland leans east, concentrated around the Grampian Mountains.

This Pilgrim Journey touches on the four great north-eastern rivers of Scotland, the Tay, the Dee, the Don and the Spey. Together they ring the Grampians while creating strategic routes through the hills, and feeding fertile lowlands beyond. The journey is therefore now Lowland and next Highland, and sometimes both together. Each of the rivers has created distinctive sites and traditions, while taken as a whole the pilgrim inheritance of the north-east is unrivalled anywhere in Britain. Why is it so neglected and little understood?

The overall scale of this Journey is epic and deliberately designed to challenge preconceptions. Yet so concentrated at points is the interest, that one stage alone repays significant investments of time and imagination. But whether by coast or glen, historic village, or cathedral church, one cannot forget the majestic silence of the mountains at the centre. The vast isolation and ecological fragility of those remote hills draws people inexorably to the mountain vision. The purity of sound and contemplation evoked ensures that however far we travel, and however busy our curiosity, something of the mystery will always elude us, carried from the mountains by those great streams of life to the sea.

MORNING

I believe that I now understand why the
Buddhist goes on pilgrimage to a mountain. It
is a journey into Being, for as I penetrate more
deeply into the mountain's life, I penetrate also
into my own. For an hour I am without desire.
The senses must be used. For the ear, the most
vital thing that can be listened to here is silence.
Always something moves. When the air is quite
still there is always running water. But now and
then comes an hour when the silence is all but
absolute, and listening to it one slips out of time.
I am not out of myself but in myself. To know
Being, this is the final grace accorded by the
mountain.
(*Nan Shepherd 'The Living Mountain'*)

BLESSING

I will lift my eyes to the mountains;
From where will my help come?
My help comes from the maker of heaven and
earth;
He will not let you stumble,
But remains awake to guard you;
He shall not sleep or be drowsy;
God is your keeper,
A shade on your right hand.
The sun will not strike you by day,

Nor the moon by night.
God will keep you from all harm,
Watching over your life;
God will guard your coming and your going
Now and for evermore.
(*Psalm 121*)

Stage 1: Perth to Braemar
By Blairgowrie

We leave Perth on the north side of the Tay heading for Old Scone. Little remains of the once magnificent Abbey, now in the grounds of Scone Palace, but the Moot Hill is still there as a reminder of this sacred site for the crowning of Scotland's kings and queens on the Stone of Destiny. Turning left off the main road towards the race course keeps you by the river and passes the perfect little Church of St David at Stormontfield. Rejoining the main road you come by the picturesque Linn of Campsie where there was once a small daughter house of Coupar Angus Abbey. At Stobhall, the old castle of the Drummonds contains a fine chapel in its courtyard. To reach the lovely secluded site of Old Cargill Church you have to go down into the village and walk to the very foot below the existing church. There was a river crossing here just below the confluence of the Isla and the Tay before there were bridges. We cross both bridges going back westwards on the other bank. Kinclaven Church, a classic Scots country kirk, is hidden on the right hand side of the road.

Continuing past Kinclaven we reach Murthly and Caputh, and then by Clunie and Kinloch to Blairgowrie. This rather neglected corner of Perthshire, on the boundary with Angus and the Grampian Mountains, is rich in Roman remains including the vast fort of Inchtuthill, which is on private land,

and the Cleaven Dyke. Next comes a wealth of forts, castles and tower houses, many associated with medieval churches and burial grounds. On the shores of Loch Clunie, on a larger mound beside the church mound, you can see the circular ramparts of Malcolm Canmore's palace, preceding the later island castle, which was built for the Bishop of Dunkeld. A few short miles west would take us to Dunkeld on the St Andrew Pilgrim Journey between Iona and St Andrews.

Blairgowrie is a busy town and route centre joined to Rattray on the other side of the strong flowing River Ericht. North of the towns is a serpent shaped Pictish mound that was the original stronghold guarding the pass north by Craighall, the present castle and mansion of the Rattrays. The road becomes steep and dramatic as it climbs into Glenshee. This is an ancient pilgrim route into the mountains. On Persie Hill at Blacklunans there was a healing well, with a traveller's hospice at Spittal of Glenshee where present day skiers congregate. East of the Spittal stands the Tomb of Diarmaid, one of the mythic comrades of Fionn, reminding us that we are entering Highland territories. Next we ascend Carnwell Pass with its Devil's Elbow, and then the gradual descent into Glen Clunie.

Coming down into Braemar, Kindrochit Castle sits above the Clunie Bridge. Founded by Malcolm Canmore, the castle was later a fortress of the Earls of Mar, like the later Braemar Castle. The whole area has a rugged hardy feel with the Celtic Earls, the Farquharsons, sometimes known as Clan Finlay, and the MacDuffs spawning martial history and legend. The 1715 Jacobite Rising began here under the Earl of Mar with a convocation of chiefs and nobles.

Given this background it is unsurprising that the early Christian missionaries did not have an easy passage. St Monire came here by Glenshee, and rested on the slopes of Morrone Hill above Braemar, where according to Gaelic tradition the Cailleach or Auld Mither dwelt milking the deer. Repulsed by the people in the village, Monire turned west into the upper Dee valley but was again driven away from Inverey. Bruised and weary he lay down on the lower slopes of Carn na Moine where he slept. Waking parched and hungry, he found a spring bubbling up and the deer grazing above it. There a priest of the old faith challenged Monire, cursing the spring, but the saint blessed it in the name of Mary and it bubbled up with redoubled force. So Monire won his first convert in the Dee valley, and St Monire's Well, also known as Tobar Mhoire, became a place of healing.

It is good to continue past Carn na Moine to the deep Linn of Dee before coming back to Braemar. Walkers might go further up to the river's source at Wells of Dee or other dramatic locations in the Braes of Mar and the Cairngorms beyond. Hardy long distance trekkers could follow the Geldie Burn, then climb over into Glenfeshie and down to the Spey. The difficulty of these journeys shows why our main route is such a vital artery.

Stage 2: Braemar to Aberdeen

Now that we have acknowledged the source, we can follow the Dee from Braemar to the 'aber' or mouth of the river at Aberdeen. This was also the direction taken by St Monire on his quest to reach the people of north-east Scotland. In Braemar itself the very fine St Margaret's Church, originally Episcopal, is developing as a cultural and pilgrimage centre. The parish church, more recently centred in the village, was originally sited a mile to the east in the Haugh of Dee, where the burial ground and a Farquharson mausoleum still stand, near Braemar Castle.

Balmoral Estate is the next main feature. The present Crathie Kirk is on the left past the Balmoral entrance, but the old church and burial ground of St Monire is to the right on lower ground by the river. Keeping to this lower road you pass on the south side of the river Abergeldie Castle, a former Gordon stronghold, and a mile further on marked by a standing stone the site of an even older Chapel of St Monire. The River Muick joins the Dee from the south and at the confluence there is another old chapel site and burial ground. Glen Muick runs south giving excellent views of Lochnagar or more properly Ben Chiochean – Hill of the Paps, another example of the ancient belief that the land was female and a goddess.

Ballater is the largest town in the mid-Dee valley with modern churches and a bustling tourist centre. To get the feel of the older Pass of Ballater take the main road back west to Bridge of Gairn, where the former chapel of St Kentigern is sited below the bridge close to the confluence of the Gairn and the Dee. Then go east again through the Pass directly to Milton of Tullich where you find the church of St Nathalan. He is the next Deeside saint, who lost faith when his efforts to help the local people came to nothing after their crops failed. He locked his working arm to his side, threw the key into the Dee and went on pilgrimage to Rome. There he met a boy who sold him a fish, and inside the fish was the key, so Nathalan returned home to Tullich where his font still stands, and where he is reputedly buried.

Keeping on the north side of the Dee we reach Aboyne where the local church dedication is to St Machar; Kincardine O'Neill which has a church and hospice for travellers coming over Cairn O Mount; and then Banchory where St Ternan founded the earliest church by the river at the east end of the present town. An attractive alternative is to go to Banchory on the south side of the river by Birse, with its old church and crusader stone, and Marywell. There are Jacobite and Roman Catholic connections here through the Farquharson and the Innes families. Back on the north side, Kincardine retains a holy well dedicated to an otherwise unknown Irish saint, Erchan.

Travelling from Banchory south of the river takes us through Kirktown of Durris to Maryculter. Here the parish church in the kirkton replaces a Templar Chapel of St Mary which was close to the Dee about a mile further west. Legend says a beautiful Saracen woman followed the Knight Godfrey of Wetherhill whom she had nursed when he was on crusade and severely wounded. But the Master of the Order had Godfrey executed because of this relationship, and scorned the lady. In consequence, he was struck down at the place by the churchyard called 'Thunder Hole'. Godfrey and his lady are buried near the Corbie Linn, where their ghosts still walk.

East of Maryculter is Blairs Castle which became a Roman Catholic seminary and latterly museum. The north-east has long surviving Roman Catholic and Episcopalian traditions alongside the Presbyterian Kirk of Scotland. Finally on this side of the river we reach Banchory-Devenick, where the last of our Deeside saints, St Devenick, is buried. We are now on the outskirts of Aberdeen where the city centre offers a range of fine churches, including the Toun Kirk of St Nicholas, and the more modern Roman Catholic Cathedral in Union Street. This side of Aberdeen is the trading town that grew up above the still bustling port at the mouth of the Dee.

Stage 3: Old Aberdeen to Fraserburgh By Old Deer

Old Aberdeen is one of the understated glories of Scottish pilgrimage, combining an early cathedral settlement with an ancient medieval university. The university stretches along the spine of Old Aberdeen, with Kings College at its centre. Founded by the great medieval bishop and Scottish patriot, William Elphinstone, Kings College has at its heart a Chapel dedicated to the Virgin Mary as Our Lady of the Nativity. The architecture consciously imitates the supposed proportions of the Temple of Solomon in Jerusalem, and the underlying philosophy is one of sacred Wisdom.

But there is more, as the High Street leads on to St Machar's Cathedral, which stands in its own Chanonry or precinct in a once secluded grove above the River Don. We know very little about Machar individually, but that may be because he was part of a movement rather than a solo trip, as we have already discovered coming down the Dee. The saints of the north-east combine Columban inspiration with a determination to ground Christianity in Pictish society and culture. Amid the many eye-catching features of St Machar's is the modern memorial to Archdeacon Barbour, author of the medieval epic poem 'The Brus'.

Crossing the Don, the journey goes north along the sandy coast to Dyce, Balmedie, Newburgh, and Collieston, past the ruins of Slains Castle, to Cruden. Stop at the Episcopal church on the hill above Cruden for a commanding view over the rolling, fertile lands of Buchan. The coast road goes on to Boddam, with its majestic lighthouse, and Peterhead, but we divert outside Peterhead inland to Old Deer. The Celtic monastery of Deer, founded by St Drostan, was probably located on the bank of the Ugie near the old parish church in the village. The medieval abbey was established by the Comyn Earl of Buchan on more spacious lines a bit upriver. Both places should be visited.

Old Deer was a centre of early scholarship and devotion, with notes on the Book of Deer exhibiting the earliest known written example of Scottish Gaelic. Drostan was an associate of Columba, but with a Pictish name and numerous foundations, he has some claim to be 'Apostle to the Picts'. The Book of Deer attributes its name to a sorrowful parting between Columba and his young follower after the Abbey had been founded. Tears – deur in Gaelic – were shed. This doubtful etymology is a fine example of the wonderful Gaelic tradition that every place name should have its story!

Peterhead is a substantial industrial port, though also an ancient burgh, with a range of churches including the remains of the original St Peter's Church on the south side of the town. Our route continues north on the coast past Inverugie with its castles, to St Fergus. This seems to be the first settlement of this Irish inspired Pictish missionary. The present St Fergus Church is a little inland, but out on the sandy flats to the north-east is the isolated, atmospheric Old St Fergus Church, redolent of the seagoing saints and their desire to find the 'place of their resurrection'. We are now set fair for Fraserburgh by way of the low lying sandy plains in which Crimond, Rattray and Lonmay are located, all with old churches. The fishing village of St Comb's flags up, like St Fergus, the seaborne Irish influence here. Lonmay Episcopal Church had as one of its ministers John Skinner, the poet and songwriter who was much admired by Robert Burns.

Stage 4: Fraserburgh to Elgin

Fraserburgh, like Peterhead, is a busy fishing harbour and industrial port, with a long history. Built on Kinnaird Head its old castle is now an impressive lighthouse. Continuing on the coastal route to Rosehearty turn left to reach Pitsligo Castle and village with its old parish church. Turning left at Peathill, we are approaching hillier ground on the borders of Buchan and Banff. On the right the hill fort of Dun Dearg has associations with Columba and Drostan, who may have established a monastery here. A little further on below New Aberdour is St Drostan's Church of Aberdour, and on the beach St Drostan's Well. The coastline becomes increasingly steep with the dramatic village of Pennan, and Troup Head which can only be reached by foot. Likewise the ancient chapel and well in the Tore of Troup which cuts inland. Next comes the fishing village of Gardenstown, and above it to the west on Gamrie More Head the precariously sited Church of St John of Gamrie. You can walk comfortably to this very complete medieval ruin, though the skulls of decapitated Danish raiders which once adorned the walls are long gone.

We are now in Banffshire proper with its string of coastal villages and towns. Banff, as the ancient county town, has an outstanding architectural heritage but sadly little of its earlier religious buildings survive. There was a Carmelite Friary, a Templar Church, and the old parish church by the harbour which retains its burial ground. Whitehills and Portsoy, with Portknockie and Findochty further west, are all attractive fishing settlements, while Macduff and Buckie are working towns and ports. An alternative to the coast is to detour south by Kirktown of Alvah, with its ancient Church and Well of St Colm, to Kirkton of Auchterless with its Church of St Donnan, and Turriff with an ancient church of St Congan. Then return west on to Aberchirder and, a little beyond, Kirkton of Marnoch. This is the same saint as Inchmarnock off Bute and Kilmarnock. His church here is built within a prehistoric stone circle. All the leading Irish missionary saints seem to have sought a presence in this region.

Our inland detour however returns south-west toward the coast by Fordyce, where the old village and its castle cluster round the even older Church and Tower of St Talorgan or Tarkin, whose only known legacy appears to be this peaceful place. Talorgan was an associate of St Donnan, and is believed to have lost his life with that saint when their home monastery on Eigg was destroyed by raiders. A little further west is located the Old Church of Deskford with its superb sixteenth-century sacrament house, and earlier features including the water stoups, aumbries and the former holy well of St John on the hillside. The Ogilvie Lairds here were close allies of Mary Queen of Scots and devoted Roman Catholics. Returning south to the coast at the historic town of Cullen, we find another fine church of St Mary endowed by the Ogilvies, a little inland of the harbour area.

Leaving Banffshire we cross into Moray reaching Elgin by way of Fochabers and Lhanbryde – the Church of Bride which was originally on the steep mound in the centre of the village. Fochabers was the headquarters of the all-powerful Gordons who long ruled most of north-east Scotland as Earls of Huntly and Dukes of Gordon. But their castle and palace here are only shadows of their erstwhile scale and magnificence. Elgin was the county town and ecclesiastical capital of this region with its magnificent, and still impressive, cathedral ruins (the Lantern of the North), the Bishop's House and the associated historic churches in and around the town. The Elgin Museum houses early carvings from many key sites in the wider area.

ON THE WAY

LANTERN OF THE NORTH

So many early fragments survive,
Clues to the places of the past,
Glimmers of a lost, early world.

But the Lantern of the North
Brings new scale, and vision.
The kingdom of Scots in Europe
Shines forth across the land
But in turn the kingdom wanes
Gives way to time's assaults.
Our journey continues on hidden tracks,
Sources of a world glimpsed
And stubbornly enduring
For us to find afresh.

BLESSING

By seashore and harbour,
By river, glen and shady dell,
By hill and strath,
May we find peace ahead,
Behind, beside, above.
Guide us in the ways of quietness
And give rest to our souls,
Even in the heat of the midday sun,
Or wind and storms from the sea
Shelter us beneath your wings.

Stage 5: Elgin to Pluscarden
By Lossiemouth, Findhorn, and Forres

Going out of Elgin north towards Lossiemouth, the
old parish church beyond the woods at Hill of Spynie

was the site of the first cathedral of the diocese. Ramsay MacDonald, the first and some would say only socialist Prime Minister of Britain, is buried here. A little further on to the right is the ruined Bishop's Palace and Castle which were once on an island, before Loch Spynie to the east was drained to its present size. After Spynie take the left fork to Kinneddar, where the old church marks the monastery of St Gerardine of Lossie. He also lived in a cave on the seafront, now lost, where he kept a lamp lit to guide sailors into harbour. So he became a saint of light and seeing. To the locals he was simply 'the Halyman'. Some fine carved stones from Kinneddar are in the Elgin Museum. Old Lossie sits at the mouth of the river with superb beaches stretching in either direction.

Keep to the coast road west of Lossiemouth where you see the Halliman Skerries, named for Gerardine, offshore. The fishing village of Hopeman comes next and then the village of Burghead, which was formerly a Pictish fort on the headland. Here beneath a cottage garden is located the superb Burghead Well. Originally a pagan sanctuary this underground chamber later became a Christian baptistery – a dramatic descent into underground darkness followed by a re-ascent to the light. The famous Burghead Bull carvings come from here and examples can be seen in Burghead Library and the Elgin Museum. The Well is unattended and keys need to be collected from the headland visitor centre or other locations in the village depending on the season.

The road goes inland across Burghead Bay to Kinloss and then Findhorn. There was a Cistercian Abbey at Kinloss, now a fragmentary ruin, and the area is better known for its modern airfield. At Findhorn by contrast the modest parish church has been outgrown by the modern Findhorn Community with its inclusive spiritual philosophy, and improvised architecture. The impressive Universal Hall at Findhorn is now a regular cultural venue for Moray. The road slips down from Kinloss to Forres by way of Sueno's Stone, an outstanding example of Pictish monumental art.

From the attractive burgh of Forres, we go southwest through Rafford and then turn left into the valley of the Blackburn for Pluscarden. The restored Abbey, now Benedictine, is a revival masterpiece, recovering a substantial medieval ruin for adapted modern use. The church is an inspiring space illuminated by stained glass made at the Abbey. An old pilgrim destination has been splendidly renewed.

Stage 6: Pluscarden to Dufftown
By Birnie, Inveravon, and Tomintoul

This epic pilgrim journey now takes a major turn into the Spey Valley. Before leaving Moray, however, we must find our way by the back roads east through Auchtertyre to Paddockhaugh where the exceptional St Brendan's Church of Birnie is sited on a small hill. This may be the oldest church in

Scotland, and its treasures include early carvings and a Celtic hand-bell – the Ronnel Bell – preserved at the manse nearby. St Brendan the Navigator himself may have established this church, and travelled over the hill to Knockando where there is a baptismal pool in the Spey named Pulvrennan – Brendan's pool. The hill route back by Dallas and then south is steep and lonely, so continuing east into Glen Rothes makes for easier travelling, by Rothes, Archiestown and Knockando, crossing the river at Marypark, to reach Inveravon.

The church at Inveravon, set above the river's junction with the Spey, is a strategic early location reputedly founded by St Drostan. There are some fine Pictish carvings on display in the church porch. From here it is possible to follow the Spey on the old missionary route by Nethybridge to Kincraig, where the church a mile south of the village was dedicated to Drostan, and Insch which has a Celtic hand-bell associated with Adomnan. That is a clue that this route can reach on westwards through Kingussie, with its original dedication to Columba, by Laggan, dedicated to Cainnech or Kenneth, to join St Columba's Pilgrim Journey on the Great Glen. But our journey is following the Avon south into the Grampians.

Glen Avon is a narrow Highland defile, scenic and populated with archaeological sites and remains. Walkers might tackle the route west of the river that climbs to the ancient church and well at Chapeltown of Kilnmachlie eventually rejoining the main road at little Bridge of Avon in the glen. West or east, the destination is the Victorianised but attractive tourist centre of Tomintoul. Distilleries abound in all directions, but on a different spiritual tack, this area is one of the few in Scotland to have a Roman Catholic tradition unbroken since medieval times, because of the protection of the Gordon Catholic nobility. This is an essential part of its distinctive character, tucked away in a network of hospitable little glens within the high mountain ranges.

This becomes even more apparent going north-west into the Braes of Glenlivet. A right turn at Auchnarrow takes us up to the road end at Chapeltown and beyond that on a track to Scalan. This was a remote, hidden seminary before nineteenth-century Catholic Emancipation allowed a gradual normalisation of the Catholic faith once more in Presbyterian Scotland. This equally scenic and remote route continues back on the main road by Glen Livet and Glen Rinnes to Dufftown.

Stage 7: Dufftown to Old Aberdeen By Huntly, Rhynie, and Chapel of Garioch

Dufftown is a whisky town, though much older in origin than its distilleries. Half a mile south at Kirktown of Mortlach is the church and early monastic settlement of St Moluag of Lismore. There is an abundance of early remains here in and around the present church, and some have argued that this is the first centre of the Diocese of Aberdeen. Whatever the history, we know that we are standing on many layers of Christian heritage by the Dullan Burn. There is no fuss or bustle here in the rural north-east, but quiet depth and meaning.

The last leg of the journey will take us back to the River Don but first we go to Keith, where the oldest church, on the east bank of the River Isla, is dedicated to St Maelrubha of Applecross, later evolving to St Rufus, as Gaelic names became more unfamiliar. Keith is a handsome town, though rivalled by our next stopping place Huntly, capital of the Gordon country. The main feature here is the dominant castle with its rich heraldic ornament, some of which has been defaced to obliterate the older Roman Catholic imagery. As previously mentioned the Gordon Earls retained their traditional Catholic allegiance. George MacDonald, founder of modern fantasy literature and inspirer of Tolkien and C.S. Lewis, was born here, and also wrote touchingly about the social and spiritual life of north-east Scotland.

The route goes on south to Rhynie, nestling below Tap o' Noth with its multiple ancient remains, including Clochmaloo, the Stone of Moluag. Cutting back towards Leith Hall, we turn south-east towards Bennachie by Insch, Oyne and Chapel of Garioch. This has been a sacred landscape since prehistoric times, devoted to the Cailleach or Auld Mither, her giant offspring, and the maiden who is turned to stone escaping from the devil. The Maiden Stone is at the roadside going from Oyne to Garioch. Christian sites and dedications cluster round with the Church of the Virgin at Chapel of Garioch looking two miles to the Mither Tap or Pap of Bennachie. Insch's dedication is to St Drostan.

Due south of Chapel of Garioch, in the Don Valley, is Monymusk where a Culdee monastery gave way to a medieval priory and then today's superb church. The famous reliquary, the Brecbennoch of St Columba, was kept here in medieval times. A jewelled casket, elaborately incised and inlaid with early Celtic deigns, the reliquary contained a bone of St Columba and was carried into battle by the Scottish army at Bannockburn. It is now has pride of place in the National Museum in Edinburgh. Like Mortlach, Monymusk is an atmospheric and many-layered location. One could travel much farther and see far less.

We follow the Don by the growing towns of Kemnay, Inverurie and Kintore back finally to Old Aberdeen at the mouth.

EVENING

Returning to the sanctuary
Of town, and the lights,
By land and sea, we are
Weary but welcome.
Content to have filled this

Day with the presence of
All that is good, long-lasting,
Precious and deep planted
In this native soil.

BLESSING

St Machar, Moluag, Maelrubha,
St Drostan, Fergus, Talorgan,
St Donnan, Adomnan, Brendan
St Monire, Ternan, Devenick,
St Mary, Peter and John,
Bless this journey to ourselves
And all whom we love,
This evening and to the world's end.

Route Four
Perthshire Circles:
The St Fillan and
St Serf Pilgrim Journey

West meets east in this twin journey through the green vales of Perthshire. From Leinster in Ireland, Fillan came with his mother Kentgerna and his uncle Comgan to Kintail in north-west Scotland. Having established a base at Kilillan, Fillan came south to Tyndrum and then into Glen Dochart. On the eastern side, Serf, a British rather than Irish Celt, established a base at Logie Airthrey near Stirling, and working his way along the Hillfoots, crossed the Ochils to Dunning in Perthshire.

Both saints have left us a legacy of stories, because they are both frontiersmen, operating at the meeting point of Irish, Pictish, British and later Germanic cultures. What unites them is a passion to ground the new faith in places of spiritual influence and power. They seeded a different future for Scotland, and command local loyalty and devotion to the present day.

However, our starting point for this journey is to the south at Dunblane which was founded by the Irish missionary, Blane. His story links with another Pilgrim Journey, St Blane and St Kessog, starting in the green island of Bute in the Clyde estuary.

MORNING

Let praise sound in bell and psalm,
Let praise sound in running streams
Let praise sound in word and birdsong
Let praise sound by art and heart
Let praise sound by faith and deed
May all creation praise its Maker.

BLESSING

May He who brought us
From the restfulness of night
To the joyous light of day,
Be bringing us also
From the new dawn of day
To the guiding light of eternity
From darkness to eternal light.

Stage 1: Dunblane to Balquhidder

Dunblane sits by a deep gorge through which the River Allan flows down to the Carse of Stirling. This creates a narrow passage between Perthshire and Stirlingshire, and between Lowlands and southern Highlands. This has led to many historic battles being fought in the area, but for Blane the point was to establish a centre of Christian community at this strategic gateway. The medieval cathedral has a commanding site above the town looking down into the gorge.

From Dunblane we continue by the town of Doune, in which the old church dedication is to Maodhag or Aodhan, better known as St Aidan. The forbidding Castle of Doune lowers over the River Teith, and from its battlements the Lady Doune, according to the ballad, looked long to see her son the Earl of Moray 'come sounding through the toun'. The wait was fruitless as Moray had been assassinated.

Past Callendar we ascend the Pass of Leny to reach Balquhidder Glen. In the village, a little off the main road, at least three successive churches on this site take us back through the centuries to St Angus, who is represented here in a primitive relief of the saint proffering a chalice. The wayward hero Rob Roy McGregor is buried here, as is the first wife of Robert Kirk, the seventeenth-century Episcopal minister, translator, and philosopher of 'The Secret

Commonwealth of Elves, Fauns and Fairies'. We are entering rich cultural territory in which the stories of the saints, the heroes of Ossian, the early clan poets, and the 'good people' (call them fairies at your peril!) intermingle.

By the time of Rob Roy in the eighteenth century the glory days of Clan MacGregor had passed, and the scattered clan had endured a hundred and fifty years of persecution. But the older poems collected by James McGregor, Dean of Lismore, remind us that they were the 'seed of Alpin', a premiere part of Scotland's Gaelic lineage, reaching far back into the age of the saints.

Stage 2: Balquhidder to Crieff
By Killin

Continuing by Lochearnhead to Killin, you find the Falls of Dochart tumbling into Loch Tay. Pushing a few miles further up the hill into Glen Dochart, you reach the West Highland Way which crosses the main road by the former St Fillan's Church. From here you can walk down to St Fillan's Priory, a medieval ruin on the site of the saint's own monastic cell. Walking further down the river you reach St Fillan's pool where the mentally ill came to bathe, before lying for a night in the chapel.

This is the territory of the Dewars of St Fillan's heritage, which has spawned one of the richest seams of Scottish legend. On his death Fillan reputedly left five sacred relics that symbolised the continuity of his work. They were his pastoral staff or crook, his bell, his arm-bone from which a sacred light shone when he wrote, his portable altar and the last manuscript which he was scribing. In addition the healing stones on which sufferers lay overnight were also preserved. The Dewars were stewards or guardians, perhaps originally 'the pilgrims', who took the relics to different places, so continuing Fillan's ministry.

Each of the relics carried an element of spiritual power or illumination. The arm-bone for example was carried by the Scottish army at Bannockburn, even though its Dewar had only brought its casing, prudently leaving the relic at home! In consequence Robert the Bruce endowed the priory of St Fillan, and each of the Dewars was given a hereditary grant of land to support their role. The survival of these relics however is not wholly a matter of legend as both the staff and the bell can be seen at the National Museum of Scotland in Edinburgh. The elaborately wrought casing of the crook is an intricate wonder. The healing stones are at the old mill in Killin which has been converted into a visitor information centre containing an excellent display about Fillan and the area's rich cultural history.

Coming back to Lochearnhead, you proceed along the south side of Loch Earn to St Fillan's. Confusingly the old Church of St Fillan, a mile to the south-east of the village near the foot of Dundurn Hill, is ascribed to another Fillan – yet surely a missionary in the tradition of his namesake. Further east at Comrie, the original church is dedicated to St Kessog. Our destination is Crieff, capital of the ancient Earldom of Strathearn and a busy market town which hosted the famous Crieff Tryst to which cattle were driven from all over the Highlands. An ancient Celtic cross can be seen in the High Street.

ON THE WAY

SAINT FILLAN'S HEALING GIFT

The oldest stories about Fillan come from Kintail where tradition holds that he was buried at Kilillan. The saint cut a hazel staff in a wood on the side of Loch Long before setting off on his travels. He was told by a wise physician to return there as he would find a great white serpent deep below the tree. And it was from this serpent that his healing power derived. The story relates that the physician desired this power for himself but that Fillan, like Finn and the Salmon of Wisdom, touched the water in which the snake was boiling and put his scalded finger in his mouth so innocently gaining the gift.

Whatever the origins, many Fillan traditions concern healing and many of the objects that continued to be associated with Fillan were believed to have healing properties. Also places blessed by Fillan were ascribed powers of healing such as a spring rising through an old hollow birch tree, which was remembered in the nineteen seventies by Duncan Matheson, a Kintail tradition bearer – 'All anyone had to do was take a drink from it and whatever was the matter with them it was said that it would cure it, and they believed that it had this power. If you believe the tales of the old folk it did this.'

BLESSING

Three palmfuls of the Trinity
keep you from every evil
The palmful of the God of Life
The palmful of the Christ of Love
The palmful of the Spirit's Peace
Three of Grace and One in Three

Stage 3: Crieff to Dunning
By Muthill and Aberuthven

You can travel directly from Crieff to Parth, passing the slight remains of Inchaffray Abbey beyond Gilmerton and visiting Fowlis Wester with its ancient Church of St Bean. Our route follows the Earn south towards Muthill which was the site of an early Celtic monastery and a significant medieval church, now roofless though retaining its tower. The area is rich in Roman remains and the name 'Moot Hill' – place of assembly – suggests somewhere more significant than the present settlement. Turning to the left onto the minor road beyond the church you soon discover how important this part of the Earn valley once was in religious terms.

Follow the signs to Innerpeffray which sits on the banks of the river, with a castle, medieval church and an ancient library. A little further on is Kinkell where the original church, in a garden opposite the more recent building, is also dedicated to Bean who seems to have been an Irish missionary working on the frontiers between the British Celts and the Picts. Kinkell is famous for its bridge and for a scandalous rhyme:

Oh what a parish, what a terrible parish,
Oh what a parish is that of Kinkell;
They hae hangit the minister, drowned the precentor,
Dang doon the steeple and drucken the bell!

An early minister was convicted of child murder and hanged at Muthill to the outrage of the parishioners who then wrought the havoc described.

Aberuthven is another ancient parish with a substantial former church just south-west of the village. It was dedicated to Blane's uncle St Catan, and is the burial place of the Dukes of Montrose, and of the local Grahams. Aberuthven is now part of Auchterarder parish where the ancient dedication is to St Kessog. Going north in the opposite direction towards Perth, turn right to Forteviot, once a great royal homestead of the southern Picts, surrounded by the fertile acres of Strathearn. Only aerial photos and the little church remain as clues to what was once here, along with the richly stone-carved Dupplin Cross, now in St Serf's Church at nearby Dunning. From Forteviot two peaceful country roads lead south to Dunning.

Stage 4: Dunning to Dunblane
By Hillfoots and Sherrifmuir

Suddenly at Dunning we reach St Serf's sphere of influence. St Serf's Church in Dunning contains early Christian carvings and a notable tower. Walking round the village you find a memorial to victims of the witch craze, the Dragon's Den where the redoubtable Serf slew a scaly monster, and on the upper side near the park a standing stone.

In Devon of his devotioun
And prayers, he slew a fell dragoun;
Where he was slain, that place was aye
The dragounis den called to this day.

A scenic road leads over the Ochils to Yetts o' Muchart on the River Devon. From here all routes are Serf's. To the east is Loch Leven where Serf founded an island monastery. A later Prior Andrew Wyntoun wrote a famous Scots Chronicle in verse which preserves many stories of the founder, including the one above.

Southwards on the Forth is Culross where Serf founded another monastery on the site of the present substantial medieval church at the top of this wonderfully conserved little town. Here Serf received the infant Mungo and his mother, who is variously named Tennoch, Thenew or Enoch. She was fleeing from the vengeful fury of her royal father Loth, and Serf's gift of sanctuary changed the history of Scotland. Also on the Forth, at Dysart, St Serf had a retreat or hermitage, which is still secluded in the grounds of a Carmelite Convent.

All of these places are visited on other Pilgrim Journeys, so for now we follow Serf west along the Hillfoots through a series of towns and churches named after this founding father, about whose early life we know next to nothing. St Serf's is the dedication at Tillicoultry, and the old church on the hillside above Alva, while to the south at Tullibody he shares that honour with his protégé Mungo or Kentigern – who also inspires the main church dedication in Alloa.

However, Serf's earliest base may have been in the lost village of Airthrey on the little road just above the present day Logie Kirk. There is an ancient church ruin here, also associated with the earlier missionary Palladius who may have inspired Serf's original choice of missionary endeavour. This little road winds steeply upwards onto Sheriffmuir providing a quiet and scenic short cut back to our starting point at Dunblane.

EVENING

Going west today the sun was rising at our back,
But now red fires subside below the western hills.
The sun has gone full circle from day into the
night,
Its last rays guide each traveller to peaceful rest.
And the light of Fillan lingers in the west
And the light of Serf waits calmly in the east.

BLESSING

Bless Thou the dwelling
And each who rests herein this night,
Bless Thou my dear ones
In each place wherein they sleep.
In the night that is tonight
And every single night,
In the day that is today
And every single day.

Route Five
Coming to the Clyde:
The St Mungo
Pilgrim Journey

Culross

Falkirk

Bar Hill

GLASGOW

Sanquhar

Dumfries

Ruthwell

Born on a beach, he united east and west, founded Glasgow, baptised Merlin, opened up the Lake District and established Britain's newest city – in Wales. All before returning to save a royal marriage and organise a Columba summit. Mungo connects Culross with Glasgow, Lanarkshire with Dumfriesshire and beyond – every place that he touched becomes a story.

Though principally remembered as Glasgow's founding saint, Mungo, who is more properly Kentigern, is one of the makers of Christian Britain. He is also the saint of stories, not only in the number of tales that attach to his name but because he deliberately set out to create a heroic Christian narrative. This was intended to replace, and in some ways to continue, the British Celtic culture in which he had been raised.

Mungo's biography itself is a story of dramatic contrast. Born to royal parents in a situation of life-threatening conflict and peril, he was educated in the refuge of a monastery, and then ventured out on his own in an enterprise that was to overturn his reverses and make history. Mungo is a childhood nickname meaning 'the dear one', but Kentigern seems to have been a formidable and, at times, intimidating character. But then, so was his mother Thenew or Enoch. Even his royal father Ewan of Strathclyde displayed a grim determination to have his own way.

MORNING

In the moment of crisis
there is also opportunity.
Sometimes the most important
decisions are instinctive:
a woman's freedom to choose,
in the teeth of adversity,
maternal passion, survival,
and the kindness of strangers.
Can we be hospitable,
receptive, far-seeing,
whatever the challenge?

BLESSING

God is our refuge and our strength,
A help to hand in any trouble.
Therefore we shall not be afraid though the earth
moves,
And mountains fall into the depth of the sea,
And waters roar and run and the mountains
quake.
There is a river, the streams of which gladden
The city of God, the holy place of the Most High.
God dwells in her midst and she will not be
moved;
God will hasten to help her at break of day.
(*from Psalm 46*)

Stage 1: Culross to Falkirk

Mungo is a pet name given to the young boy whom St Serf fostered at his monastery at Culross. Serf was apostle to the Hillfoots, and over the Ochils to Dunning. He gave refuge to Mungo's mother when she was washed up on the beach and birthed her child beside a fire the monks had built there.

But this baby's real name was Kentigern. His mother was a British princess, his father a royal prince of Strathclyde. His grandfather was the last pre-Christian ruler of Lothian, while his grand-mother was reputed to be a niece of the great King Arthur himself. Thenew, the single mother who is also known as Tennoch or Enoch, had been cast adrift on the Forth estuary, but landed on the Isle of May and caught the tide upriver.

Visit Culross Abbey above the town and imagine a growing boy whose grace overcame all his class-mates' jealousy, even restoring to life Serf's pet robin whom they had carelessly killed. Serf thought Mungo would be his successor and was heartbroken when the young man crossed the Forth at Kincardine in response to his own missionary calling. Near present-day Cowie at Kearnach or Carnock, Mungo tended a holy man named Fergus and, in obedience to his dying wish, set him on a cart drawn by two bulls, who headed west.

The route of Mungo's journey was close to the Antonine Wall which commences at Boness and

Falkirk. Near the mouth of the Carron, the Helix Kelpies with their dramatic rearing heads are like the horses of Manaan, god of the sea. Following the Falkirk Wheel and the Forth–Clyde Canal locks, you mark the wall's route. To visit the town of Falkirk itself you divert south.

The birth and childhood of Kentigern are in themselves a romance tale. Up against it, when hope and will were all that remained to win through, Thenew, and then Mungo himself, showed true faith and courage.

May we come ashore
Where freshwater springs assuage our salt thirst
May we find the courage
To put out once more into the currents,
Trusting in the kindness
Of strangers who may host angels unawares.

Stage 2: Falkirk to Glasgow

There is a close connection between Roman remains and the struggle in Mungo's time to restore the inheritance of early British Christianity. Modan, the saint of Falkirk, is another figure in this movement whose storytellers, including Mungo, turned the Celtic hero Arthur into a Christian warrior, champion of Romano-Christian Britain when the Romans had gone. Walkers and cyclists can go up to the Antonine

Wall midway fort at Barhill above Twechar to catch something of the frontier atmosphere.

By Bonnybridge, Kilsyth and Kirkintilloch, Mungo entered the region of St Ninian's earlier influence. In a burial ground beside the Molendinar dedicated to Ninian, Mungo laid Fergus to rest, and decided to start a community in this 'dear green place'. The medieval glories of Glasgow Cathedral lay far ahead. What is now the Necropolis hill was a fortified citadel, and legend has Merlin, prophet of the old beliefs, hurling insults at the nascent Christian settlement below. Later accounts portray Mungo as a John the Baptist figure, dressed in goatskins with a fisherman's cowl and striding out with a rough staff rather than an ornamental crozier. He was 'the warrior of God' battling through tough times.

Nonetheless Mungo's founding inspiration is maintained through every phase of this beautiful Cathedral's life. The Blackadder Aisle, which depicts the transporting of Fergus, may be built over the original burial ground. St Enoch or Thenew's Well is in the lowest level of the building close to where the Molendinar once ran. And though the shrine behind the high altar, which housed the Saint's relics, is long gone, the Chapel of St Mungo in the crypt is his place of burial. They are all places fit for pilgrimage. Glasgow's coat of arms, with its bird, bell, tree and fish, is based on stories from Mungo's life, and the city's motto acknowledges its founding purpose.

ON THE WAY

Let Glasgow flourish by the preaching of his
word
and the praising of his name.
Are our cities still communities, places of
solidarity,
imagination, moral and spiritual value?
Or are we in a wasteland of lost potential,
a dark age of greed, inequality and oppression?

WHEN COLUMBA MET MUNGO

When Columba heard about the fiery apostle
of Glasgow he was keen to meet Mungo in the
flesh. Often when Columba travelled he would
go alone or with a few companions, but on this
occasion the community insisted on a strong
turnout with some appropriate holy books and
precious treasures to show how important Iona
and its Abbot were in Scotland.
When Mungo heard about Columba's visit
he too was very curious to meet the great
apostle of Ireland. Equally his community at
Glasgow was determined to put on a good
show, demonstrating their importance. So some
processional banners and special vestments were
prepared for the forthcoming summit.
Of course, as ever, politics were at play here too,
since Scotland was still divided into different

peoples and kingdoms. Glasgow was in the British Celtic kingdom of Strathclyde, while Iona was on the boundary between Dalriada in Argyll and the kingdoms of the Picts. How would the influence of this new faith play out in local politics? Which kingdoms and whose holy apostles would take precedence?

The big day came and messengers arrived at the Molendinar river to breathlessly announce Columba's approach. The Glasgow procession set out led by Mungo carrying his sacred staff of office. Meanwhile of course the Iona delegation had formed into a ceremonial procession led by their Abbot with his sacred staff or crook.

Many people had gathered to watch, intrigued no doubt to see who would defer to whom. Who would give way and pay homage, as worldly kings would expect?

The two processions approached from different sides. Hand-bells were rung and horns blown. They came to a stop as if by mutual consent about twenty yards from each other. Silence fell as the two saints looked across the short distance. Both were simply dressed and bareheaded with their crooks resting on the ground in their right hands. Then at the same moment Columba and Mungo walked towards each other, alone. Coming close, at the exact same instant, they held out their crooks to each other and the staffs were exchanged, giving with the right and receiving with their left hands. And then staffs still in hand

they embraced each other as brothers, and
children equal in God's sight.

As their arms unfolded a huge smile lit up their
faces, and the people cheered and shouted their
approval. Each of the two great apostles had
met in the other a kindred spirit to esteem and
cherish.

BLESSING

Blessed are the peacemakers
And the pure at heart
And those who hunger
And thirst for justice,
Blessed are those
Persecuted for the right
And falsely accused
In the cause of Christ
For they are children
Of the kingdom of love.
(*The Beatitudes*)

Stage 3: Glasgow to Ruthwell

Unsurprisingly, Mungo was soon at odds with the
local establishment. Clashing with Morkan, ruler of
the day, he had to move south into the Clyde valley,
leaving his monastery at Glasgow still in the making.
By Rutherglen, Cambuslang, Blantyre, Bothwell, and

Hamilton, you visit proud, distinctive communities which have been drawn into the Greater Glasgow conurbation, while retaining their own character and heritage. On the route are Bothwell Collegiate Church, the David Livingstone Centre at Blantyre and Hamilton Old Parish Church.

Following the lovely Clyde valley to Lanark, you enter one of Scotland's oldest towns, dramatically sited above the river. Beyond the High Street is the Church of St Kentigern in which William Wallace first met the love of his life, Marion Braidfute. The bell of St Kentigern's now hangs in the Town Kirk of St Nicholas, with its prominent statue of Wallace, the local and national hero.

Southwards is a harder, hillier landscape, softened only by the river flats. The spirit of Mungo the Baptist persists here in the sturdy medieval parish churches, and on the hillsides where Presbyterian Covenanters later held outlawed field preachings in the name of religious liberty. Roman Catholic tradition is also missionary in these parts, as the dispossessed of the nineteenth-century Irish famine sought a better life toiling in mills and mines. The persecuted of every tradition are remembered – Mungo himself had to flee further west into Nithsdale to escape his pursuers.

Between Abington and Crawford, beneath Iron Age and Roman Forts, the lost Chapel of St Constantine in its shady grove at Kirkton reminds us how this route kept a passage open for the new faith – St Constantine is remembered at Govan. Above Moffat, at the Chalybeate Well, Merlin fled to seek refuge in madness, and was later baptised by Mungo over the Devil's Beeftub on the banks of the Tweed.

Continuing by Lockerbie, scene of the worst peacetime atrocity in Scotland since the Glencoe Massacre, and Ecclefechan, birthplace of Thomas Carlyle, we go west again to Hoddom. It seems quiet here now in the old kirkyard by the river, but Mungo preached from this early Christian settlement, and through him the influence of Hoddom reached to the Lake District and west to Whithorn.

Stage 4: Ruthwell to the Lakes and St Asaph

Before his eventual return to Glasgow, under the protection of King Roderick of Strathclyde, Mungo left Scotland and journeyed through Cumbria by Penrith and Maryburgh to what is now called the Lake District. Though Cumbria was a British territory like Strathclyde, the mountainous Lakes were still wild country. From Ruthwell our journey offers a return to Glasgow by Nithsdale, or this much longer route south to Wales and Bardsey Island.

Mungo or Kentigern's progress is marked by early sites and dedications beginning from his field preaching at Keswick close to the stone circle at Castle Craig. His journey goes through the heart of the Lakes by Grasmere, Rydal, Windermere and Kendal. Mungo then continues south by Preston and Lancaster but his destination may always have been Wales, drawn by the influence of St David and the hope of Christian sanctuary.

After some initial hostility, Mungo established a monastery in North Wales at St Asaph which flourished peacefully as a longstanding Christian community, beside another River Clwyd. It was with some reluctance that after many happy years Mungo returned to the struggle in Glasgow at Roderick's request, appointing Asaph his successor.

This area remains an attractive focus of pilgrimage, coming into Wales by Chester and to the little Cathedral St Asaph via Holywell. The route then continues west by Angelsey and the Lleyn Peninsula to Bardsey Island. Perhaps Mungo would have preferred to head in that direction, but some of his most important achievements still awaited him in the north.

A later pilgrim, the Jesuit Gerard Manley Hopkins, records his sense of beauty and spiritual sanctuary here in 'In the Valley of the Elwy'.

I remember a house where all were good
To me, God knows, deserving no such thing:
Comforting smell breathed at very entering,
Fetched fresh, as I suppose, off some sweet wood.
That cordial air made these kind people a hood
All over, as a bevy of eggs the mothering wing
Will, or mild nights the new morsels of spring:
Why, it seemed of course; seemed of right it should.
Lovely the woods, waters, meadows, combes, vales,

All the air things wear that build this world of
Wales;
Only the inmate does not correspond:
God lover of souls, swaying considerate scales,
Complete thy creature dear O where it fails,
Being mighty a master, being a father and fond.

Stage 5: Ruthwell to Nithsdale and Glasgow

At Ruthwell, the astonishing carved cross unites
the worlds of Cuthbert, Mungo and Ninian. The
Dream of the Rood becomes flesh – or at least
stone. This is one of the master artworks of missionary Christianity, now sheltered in Ruthwell Parish
Church. By the Solway coast you then continue west
to Dumfries. In addition to the town's handsome
historic churches, Sweetheart Abbey nestles by the
Nith close to the estuary. On the northern outskirts
are the ruins of Lincluden Priory, famous for Robert
Burn's summer poem 'Ca the Yowes'.

Mungo came into Nithsdale to escape the ire of
his royal adversary Morkan. Follow the river north
through Burns country to Auldgirth and Thornhill.
In Upper Nithsdale a shepherd gave Mungo refuge and in return the saint educated the shepherd's
son. In due course, Conall returned to Nithsdale
as pastor and missionary to his home country. He
founded churches at lonely Kirkbride, at Sanquhar
and at Kirkland above modern Kirkconnel. He is

buried where he first met Mungo, on the hill above Glenwharry. A Celtic cross marks the place from which he could look out over the rugged scenes of his later missionary labours.

The hill theme continues back to Sanquhar and then over high ground east to Crawfordjohn, a notable Covenanting stronghold during the seventeenth-century religious conflicts. A few miles north, divert to Douglas with its medieval Church of St Bride. Then rejoin the main route north by Lesmahagow, and Kirkmuirhill. Eventually Mungo was able to return this way from exile, and Glasgow flourished again under the protection of Roderick, a new Christian ruler.

To this later period belong the Saint's labours on behalf of Roderick's wayward Queen, as he recovered her lost ring from a magnificent Clyde salmon. As described above, Columba also came to Glasgow to pay his respects and the two charismatic leaders exchanged staffs as a sign of mutual respect and communion. Glasgow had truly arrived.

EVENING

Taking the long view –
time for memory and reflection
on what has passed
where we are now
and what it may mean
for the next stage in our journey.

Mungo retraces his footsteps
the same but changed.
This the bird that never flew
The bell that never rang
The fish that never swam
The tree that never grew.
In the mystery of faith
The grace of divine love,
May we grow, fly, ring,
And swim as the salmon
Leaps from the ocean
Home to source the river
Of renewing life.

BLESSING

May you receive grace and peace
After your travelling.
And the blessing of this Cathedral
In its heights and in its depths,
In its colours and in its shadows,
Through open arches and in sheltered aisles,
Be upon you, and stay with you tonight.
And may the blessing of our founder Mungo,
Kentigern the dear one, child of Heaven's Kingdom,
Be always with you wherever you go.

Route Six
Bute to the Trossachs:
The St Blane and
St Kessog Pilgrim Journey

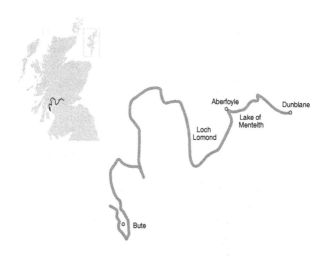

Aberfoyle

Dunblane

Lake of
Menteith

Loch
Lomond

Bute

Bute sits like a pendant jewel in the Firth of Clyde. It has been described as 'Scotland in miniature' because the Highland fault which reaches across the country runs through the island, dividing its hilly northern from its gentler southern parts. However, the overwhelming impression of Bute is one of green fruitfulness, making it a nursery of Scotland's early Celtic saints. Bute and its little acolyte isle Inchmarnock both recall the green Island of the Saints that St Brendan the Navigator visits on his famous dream voyage. St Brendan, rather than Blane, was the traditional patron saint of Bute.

Nonetheless this Pilgrim Journey is a cross-country matter, venturing over sea, loch and long south-stretching promontories into the heart of mainland Scotland. Bute is strategically placed for travel between Ireland and Scotland, becoming a welcome sanctuary and transit point on routes east. St Blane was born in Ireland on the instructions of his uncle, Catan, but returned to undertake this journey, as did St Kessog, though from a starting point slightly further north on the Cumbraes.

Yet the route is not arduous. Something of the gentle spirit of Bute and of Luss on Loch Lomond, which Kessog made his base, breathes through the landscapes of southern Argyll and of the Trossachs. This is green, moist country, whether by loch or on hill, and the Irish missionaries must have felt at home and at peace here. Both Blane and Kessog were healers, associated to this day with wells, springs and herbs.

This journey also connects up with the Perthshire routes through its final destination point at Dunblane, where the Cathedral remains an enduring monument to Blane's vision.

MORNING

O happy passing of Blane!
Let Bute rejoice above all other islands
To have sent forth a dweller with the angels.
By him the Lord's house shines with miracles.
As light shines from a golden candlestick
So Blane shone, longing for things eternal.
Glowing lamp of charity, raised high and bright,
O bountiful Blane, give us the oil of kindness
Give us the light of grace, cleansing us from sin,
leading us to the everlasting kingdom of light.
(*Aberdeen Breviary, adapted*)

BLESSING

May we walk with reverence,
for the ground we tread is holy.
May we talk with discretion,
for the way we travel is ancient.
May we listen with joy to the songs of the
stones,
And receive with gratitude the whispers of
Creation,
Waymarkers of the Spirit, Paths of Mindfulness,
Blessed Trinity, be our Guide, past, present,
future –
Three dimensions, one life journey.

Stage 1: Rothesay and the Isle of Bute

A complete circuit of Bute is a rewarding and compact experience. Rothesay itself is an attractive holiday port whose ancient Church of St Mary was at
one time a Cathedral of the Southern Isles, just as its
castle was a royal Stewart stronghold. Going north-
west first, by Port Bannatyne, you reach Kilmichael
which manages, with its ruined chapel, to feel remote,
even on Bute. Everywhere on this west coast seems
to be connected with Kintyre and Ireland.

Travelling south again, keeping to the west side,
past the lovely Ettrick Bay where Norse raiders
came ashore, we reach St Ninian's Bay where, on
the northern point, there was a substantial Celtic
monastery founded in the earliest phase of Ninian's
mission from Whithorn. This is still an evocative
place, looking out on Inchmarnock – Marnoc's or
Ernoc's Isle – whose fertile acres were home to
another early Celtic community. Here missionaries
and pilgrims found peace, but also the natural fruits
of land and sea which they regarded as the generous
gifts of their own maker.

These open outlooks contrast with the more
enclosed terrain of the south end, where there is
a rich concentration of early settlement, beyond
Kilchattan Bay. Standing stones and a stone circle
mark the approach, with Dunagoil Fort located to
the south-west and Garroch Head at the tip. Tucked
within this landscape between St Catan's Seat (Suidhe

Catain) and St Blane's Hill is the monastery and later chapel of Blane. The site is one of the most complete in Scotland, retaining its enclosing circular wall, its well and an earlier, perhaps ritual feature, the Devil's Cauldron. The sense of enclosure and shelter is remarkable, the restfulness palpable.

Coming back on the east side, the Chapel and well of Catan were at the north end of the bay, rather than the location of the present village to the south. The Ascog Fernery is a reminder of Bute's fecundity and mild climate. On the road back to Rothesay is Mountstuart, a Gothic Revival masterpiece created by the artistic passion and religious devotion of the third Marquess of Bute. His conversion to Roman Catholicism rocked Victorian society, but Pluscarden Abbey, Falkland Palace, Dunblane Cathedral and Whithorn Priory, in addition to St Blane's, were all to benefit from his determination to recover lost aspects of Scotland's spiritual heritage.

Stage 2: Rothesay to Luss
By Kilmun

Go due north from Rothesay by Kames to reach the Colintraive ferry over to Cowal. This wide hill-girt peninsula of Cowal is remarkable for the number of early Christian sites still occupied by present day churches, including Kilfinan, Kilmodan and the Church of the Three Holy Brethren at Lochgoilhead.

By contrast, north of Colintraive, Fearnoch Chapel, set in a hidden dell 500m west of the main road, is a fine example of Cowal's many lost religious sites.

Our route, however, goes east towards the Holy Loch on which are sited Cowal's main port and holiday town at Dunoon, and the ancient religious settlement of Kilmun. 'Mun' is an abbreviation of Finntan (in Irish Fiontan) Munnu, an important early saint who came to Iona after Columba's death, but stayed on in Argyll to found churches in his own right. There are other Kilmuns in Argyll, all associated with Clan Campbell, which suggests that Fintan Munnu may have been the patron saint of that clan before the conversion of their chiefs to Protestantism. This Kilmun, however, was the saint's major foundation and a centre of early learning, surviving later as the parish church. According to one account Fintan Munnu became a leper, 'a warrior, religious, and tortured with pain'. He was buried in north Argyll, in the lovely island in Loch Leven named Eilean Munde.

The journey continues by Loch Eck and the Benmore gardens to Strachur, and to St Catherine's and Kilmorich Church at Cairndow. Just off this route, at the junction with Hell's Glen road to Lochgoilhead, is the Tinker's Heart, a pattern of white quartz stones, celebrated by Scotland's Travelling People as a place of meeting and ceremony. Staying with this road offers a scenic short cut to Rest and Be Thankful or a diversion to Lochgoilhead. The main route continues by Ardkinglas through Glen Croe to Arrochar, then Tarbet and on to Loch Lomond. We have reached the land of Kessog.

ON THE WAY

THREE CHILDHOOD DRAMAS

Blane's Uncle Catan was the first to make Bute his missionary base. Coming from Bangor in County Down, he brought his sister Bertha to help establish the new community at Kilchattan. Early Celtic monasteries often included men and women, and Bertha seems to have been a strong person in her own right.

But Bertha attracted the attentions of Aedan, King of Dalriada, who was curious about the new arrivals. He came visiting and fell for Bertha. She became pregnant and was sent back to Ireland. In some versions of the tale she was cast adrift with her newborn son in a currach without oar or rudder, but this is a traditional motif in such tales, and the truth may be less dramatic.

In Ireland Bertha was received kindly by two other important saints, Congan and Kenneth. They arranged for the little boy, Blane, to be cared for and educated at Bangor. From the start, his consuming ambition was to return to Scotland, which he eventually did, working under, and then succeeding, Catan.

Marnock, or Ernan, was a young boy in the great Irish monastery of Clonmacnois, when Columba came visiting. Anxious to show the ageing saint honour and respect, the Abbot ordered a canopy to be carried above Columba's head sheltering him from rain or sun. The procession was duly making its way towards the monastery when a small boy was found hiding in the canopy and clinging to the saint's cloak.

The hosts grabbed the little boy to hustle him away but Columba stopped them. 'Put out your tongue,' he said to the child. 'Ah,' exclaimed the great man, 'this boy has a gift of eloquence and will himself become a saint of the Church.' The little boy was Ernoc.

Kessog too came from Ireland, where his father was one of the kings of Munster. When he was a teenager two other kings came to visit, both bringing their sons, hoping for some kind of sport or entertainment, as the land was in the grip of winter. The three boys set out to play, but unfortunately the two guests fell through ice on the river and were drowned.

The servants rushed to tell Kessog's father, fearful that this tragedy might bring war on Munster. And in fact the two visiting chiefs swore to avenge their sons' deaths. But Kessog took no part in these altercations, staying instead by the river to pray. When morning came the boys were found in the huts where they had been laid out for burial, coming to, dazed but alive.

BLESSING

Unexpected turnings on the road
Memories return changed by time.
What were the experiences, the moments,
The people who changed our direction.
May we be open to the unexpected,
The new, the changing perspective
That puts everything in a new light.

Stage 3: Luss to Aberfoyle

Kessog, like Blane, began life in Ireland, and the old association between the saint and the Cumbraes suggests that he may also have begun his Scottish adventure in the Firth of Clyde. However he quickly established himself at Luss, which became his headquarters, along with Inchtavannach, or Monk's Island, nearby in Loch Lomond.

From Luss, Kessog's influence spreads out into the Trossachs and Perthshire. Fairs were held in his honour at Callander and Comrie, with church dedications at Luss, Callander, Auchterarder and as far afield as the Beauly Firth, where the saint is credited with a miraculous rescue at the Kessock ferry crossing, now replaced by the Kessock Bridge.

There are strong connections between Kessog and streams, springs and herbs. 'Luss' means herb and, according to one tradition, when the saint was martyred far away his body was brought back to Luss, preserved for burial by being wrapped in herbs. More reliably, however, the saint was murdered for his faith about a mile south of Luss, where a cairn was erected. When this was taken down at the end of the eighteenth century it was found to contain a stone head representing Kessog and a statue of an early Bishop, Robert Colquhoun. The clan Colquhoun, who still own the lands of Luss, were the hereditary guardians of Kessog's relics.

Kessog, like Columba, is a saint who has gained a modern following. The present day church in Luss, which houses a medieval effigy of the saint, is a popular attraction for visitors and pilgrims. The manse glebe has a Kessog walk, where the river flows into Loch Lomond, and neighbouring churches such as the Roman Catholic parish at Balloch have also revived Kessog devotions. Glen Luss above the village was the site of a healing well dedicated to St Bride.

Our Journey follows Kessog westwards by Gartocharn, Drymen and Gartmore to Aberfoyle.

Stage 4: Aberfoyle to Dunblane

Aberfoyle is gateway to the most beautiful parts of the Trossachs, but it has its own distinctive religious associations. The local saint is Bearachan who founded his church by the ancient fortress of Aberfoyle, just where the old church and manse still stand. Later, the seventeenth-century Episcopalian priest and scholar Robert Kirk was buried here in his own churchyard, after supposedly being abducted by the 'Good People'. This may have been because Kirk had gained too much knowledge of their ways, which he put to good use in his philosophic disquisition on spiritual beliefs – 'The Secret Commonwealth of Elves, Fauns and Fairies'. Kirk was a Gaelic scholar of repute, sustaining the old link between the Church and Celtic culture. Reputed to be the seventh son of a seventh son, tradition endowed him with the gifts of a seer, and he was interested in the Highland gift of 'second sight'.

A detour further north into the Trossachs is an attractive route to Callander, but our pilgrim journey goes eastwards to Port of Menteith, from where you can cross by boat to Inchmahome. This island sanctuary – later a medieval priory – is another of Scotland's remarkable hidden places, on a par with Blane's monastery at Kingarth on Bute. The original founder was a follower of Columba, but the location close to the island headquarters of the Celtic Earls of Menteith ensured the site's ongoing importance. Later, the five-year-old Mary Queen of Scots was given refuge here with her four accompanying Marys before they were sent for safety to France. Robert Cunningham Graham, the vivid writer and radical politician who was Laird of nearby Gartmore, is buried here along with many earlier dignitaries, known and unknown. The priory ruins are shaded by mature trees and the island is deeply meditative and peaceful, lapped by the soft waters of Scotland's only natural lake. In Graham's own words,

The Isle of Rest still seems to float upon the lake. In the green sedges wild ducks settle with a whirr of wings, and in the shallows pike lie basking in the sun. The hills still are reflected in the frosted, silver mirror of the lake, as in a mirage. The monks who built the long, grey church, sleep all forgotten, unconscious that they wove the spell that still enchants the island and the lake.

Turning left beyond Menteith onto the road to Callendar, the route then returns by Doune to Dunblane. Blane's Celtic settlement may have been on the hill above the medieval Cathedral, which is poised impressively over the town and the Allan gorge. Surrounding the cathedral is Old Churches House (formerly Scottish Churches House), the Cathedral Museum and Archbishop Leighton's Library, evidencing a rich tradition of Christian thought and worship in this place. The twentieth-century restoration of Dunblane Cathedral is a significant cultural and ecumenical achievement that sustains a living spiritual heritage.

EVENING

This day has been full of places,
Diverse scenes and spaces;
Evening brings calm reflection
Night's peace and new direction.
Let nothing of this day be lost
Let everything be kept through love.

BLESSING

In the love of God,
In the affection of God,
In the will of God,
In the eye of God,
In the purpose of God,
In the care of God.
As your own angels
As your own saints
As your own household
Rest in heaven,
So may we rest on earth.

Route Seven
Forth to Tay:
The St Margaret
Pilgrim Journey

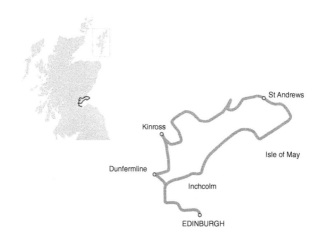

St Andrews

Kinross

Isle of May

Dunfermline

Inchcolm

EDINBURGH

St Margaret's is a pathway on which power, wealth and privilege are set aside in favour of living out Christ's commandments in letter and spirit. Educated at the Court of Edward the Confessor in London, Margaret was exceptionally well read and raised in an environment of enlightened devotion and charity.

Nonetheless, she was at the centre of Europe's royal establishment, and was made a dispossessed refugee by William the Conqueror's victory at Hastings in 1066. Whether by chance or design, she arrived by sea in Scotland, where she was welcomed by Malcolm Canmore, King of Scots. This perilous flight became the beginning of a new life for Margaret, and for Scotland. The descendants of Malcolm and Margaret were the rulers of Scotland in her medieval golden age, and kings and queens of England.

More significantly for our purposes, Margaret is the first of Scotland's saints to be officially canonised by the Pope in Rome. She is also rare among saints in being a wife and mother. Nonetheless, throughout her life she balanced her charitable and family work with a desire for seclusion and contemplation. Margaret strongly supported devotion to the Celtic saints while also connecting Scotland with the Europe-wide development of monasticism.

MORNING

Alone with none but thee, my God,
I journey on my way;
What need I fear when thou art near,
O King of night and day?
More safe am I within thy hand,
Than if a host around me stand.

Torn from home, you embrace another
You became Queen and Mother,
The Glory of Scots,
Your Queen's crown a crown of Charity,
Your Way, the Royal Way of the Cross
Blessed are all those who follow in your path.
(*Canonisation of St Margaret*)

BLESSING

The grace of Margaret
be on our journey,
And the love of Margaret
be in our hearts
For where charity and love are,
there God makes his dwelling.

Stage 1: Edinburgh

Margaret remains in the centre of Edinburgh's sacred places. At the highest point of the Castle stands St Margaret's Chapel. In the midst of the panoply of war and military might, this is a pearl of pure devotion. The Chapel was probably built by Margaret's son David on the site of his mother's place of prayer. From the Castle you can follow a Royal Pilgrim Way to Holyrood Abbey, which David founded in honour of his mother's ebony cross – the haly rude. Beyond the Abbey and the new Scottish Parliament is St Margaret's Well in Holyrood Park. The well housing was originally part of St Triduana's Well at Restalrig. The area is full of natural springs leading to a major brewing industry here, begun by the monks.

En route, on the Royal Mile, are a series of important churches including St Giles Cathedral, Old St Paul's Episcopal Church, St Patrick's Roman Catholic Church, and the Kirk of the Canongate, which was built as a successor to Holyrood Abbey Church when James VII and II wished to convert it into his Chapel Royal. The Abbey Church itself is now an evocative ruin in the grounds of Holyroodhouse Palace, but beyond the east and west ends of Princes Street are St Mary's Roman Catholic and St Mary's Episcopal Cathedrals both of which continue St Margaret's traditions. Margaret's inspiration is carried forward through worship but also through education and social action.

Many in Scotland continue to ask for the grace and humility to follow in Margaret's Way of prayer and compassionate action.

Stage 2: Edinburgh to Dunfermline By Queensferry

The River Forth is profoundly connected with Margaret's story. Here she arrived on the north shore as a storm-tossed refugee. Later, she founded the Queen's Ferry to give pilgrims safe passage to the shrine of St Andrew, whom she especially honoured as one of the first disciples. At South Queensferry, the Priory Church of St Mary of Mount Carmel marks the pilgrim hostel above the original landing stage. Nowadays boats leave from the pier at the other end of the village, from where you can sail to Inchcolm Island and Abbey (see Dunfermline to Dysart below). You can cross the river by road or rail to North Queensferry and then on to Dunfermline.

In Margaret's time Dunfermline was the capital of Scotland and her first home here. Among the atmospheric riches are the remains of the palace, the inspirational Benedictine Abbey founded by Margaret, and the enlarged Abbey Church where Robert the Bruce is buried. Amid this large scale splendour you can still find, accessed from the town centre car park, St Margaret's Cave where the saintly Queen sought solitude and contemplation amid the duties of Court life and her own efforts on behalf of the poor, the hungry, orphans and prisoners of war. Margaret was buried at Dunfermline Abbey alongside her husband Malcolm, but when a new shrine was built after her official canonisation, the coffin could not be shifted until Malcolm's was also moved. The town of Dunfermline has many fine churches in addition to the Abbey and an excellent heritage centre at Abbot's House.

From Dunfermline you can travel to St Andrews inland or by the coast. We shall describe both routes and you may choose to use both though going in different directions.

Stage 3: Dunfermline to Falkland By Loch Leven

St Margaret honoured the older Celtic traditions while also encouraging the best of modern European monasticism. Loch Leven brings these worlds together. At Kinross, at the head of the promontory is an ancient chapel and burial ground looking out to the island where Mary Queen of Scots was imprisoned in Lochleven Castle. Coming back along the near side of the loch you look out from Vane Farm Nature Reserve to St Serf's Island where a Culdee monastic refuge was succeeded by a medieval priory, of which little is now visible. Further on you reach the village of Scotlandwell with its remarkable healing well. There was a major pilgrim hostel here which has disappeared, and historic Portmoak

Church is sited at the other end of the village. If time allows, a full circuit of Loch Leven by foot, bicycle or car is a rewarding experience.

Continuing to Falkland, the hunting palace of the Stewart Kings here has been magnificently restored with a Roman Catholic Chapel, associated with Mary Queen of Scots. This is another of the restorations supported by the Marquess of Bute and the Crichton Stuart family.

ON THE WAY

Amidst land you find
a lake of Galilee
Amidst modern buildings you find
ancient sanctuary
Amidst the noisy clamour
you discover inner solitude and quiet,
Amidst Celtic hermits
Margaret found simplicity of heart.

SAINT MARGARET'S PATH

There was once a Princess called Margaret, which means 'the pearl'. She was born an exile in Hungary, daughter of a Saxon Prince and a Hungarian Princess. When Margaret's father came home to England, she was brought up at the court of the pious and learned king, Edward

the Confessor. There for the first time she met
Malcolm of Scotland who had fled from the
clutches of Macbeth.

When Edward died without an heir confusion
and war followed. The new King, Harold, was
killed at Hastings by William the Conqueror. A
fugitive once more, Margaret set sail for Hungary
but was driven by a storm to the shores of
Scotland. Malcolm, now King of the Scots, came
to meet her at what is still called St Margaret's
Bay. He fell in love and asked Margaret to
become his Queen.

Longing for the peace and holy quiet of the
cloister, Margaret hesitated to marry the warrior
king. Then she became Malcolm's wife and
Scotland's Queen.

From the beginning she opened her arms to
the people. Orphans were taken into the royal
palace, the sick and the suffering tended,
prisoners of war released, and the poorest fed.
In Malcolm's eyes, Margaret could do no wrong.
He supported her work and rewarded those who
followed her example. He would take her precious
books in his hands, turning over the pages and
kissing them. Once Malcolm sent for a jeweller to
ornament a book with gold and gems. Then he
gave it to Margaret as a token of his love. The royal
couple had two daughters and six sons, whose
upbringing was Margaret's special concern.

But Margaret also lived a secret life of prayer.
From the palace at Dunfermline she would

retreat to a cave to be alone with God, and at Edinburgh Malcolm built a chapel for her devotions. This extraordinary queen lived the ideal of inward poverty.

BLESSING

May the pure flowing waters
refresh you,
May light dancing on the waves
cleanse your vision,
May the peace of islands
surround you like an inland sea,
May deep springing wells
assuage your thirst
and satisfy your soul.

Stage 4: Falkland to St Andrews

Under the influence of Margaret and her sons, three of whom became King of Scots in turn, the medieval Church became the centre of Scottish cultural and social, as much as religious, life. This can be seen in the shape of the towns and villages, going by Cupar or by Ceres. The last inland leg is a journey through the farmlands, villages, towns and churches that have characterised north-east Fife since medieval times.

On one such journey Margaret's illuminated Gospel manuscript fell into a river – perhaps the Eden. Later it was recovered from the river bed substantially undamaged. A Gospel manuscript which is known to have belonged to Margaret is kept in Oxford's Bodleian Library and it has water markings on it. Many of Margaret's journeys had a charitable purpose, such as improving the care of children and of the poor, or seeking the release of prisoners of war. Some were pilgrimages and others were connected with the movement of the royal court about the country.

Stage 5: Dunfermline to Dysart
By the Coast of Fife

Explore what has been called the 'Columban Corridor' linking Iona to its daughter house at Lindisfarne in Northumbria. St Adomnan, Abbot of Iona, founded a monastery on Inchkeith Island, while on neighbouring Inchcolm, Margaret's son Alexander, who was given shelter on the island in a storm by a Celtic hermit, initiated what became the 'Iona of the East'. Here a later Abbot, Walter Bower, compiled his monumental History of Scotland, *Scotichronicon*, which delights in the stories of Margaret and the Celtic Saints.

Inchcolm can be reached on the Maid of the Forth from South Queensferry, though it is much closer to this northern shore. The north coastal route is studded with port towns and historic churches from the pilgrim friary at Inverkeithing through Dalmeny, Aberdour, Burntisland, Kinghorn and Kirkcaldy to

Dysart. Named for St Serf's refuge or 'desert place', Dysart is now a handsome village with a ruined Church of St Serf by the harbour. St Serf's Cave is still secluded within the grounds of a Carmelite Community.

All along the coast the views across to Edinburgh and seawards down the firth are exceptionally fine. The bustle of modern commerce and pleasure craft on the water remind us that the paths of the Celtic saints were often seaways, and that many later pilgrims travelled by ferry under the protection of St Margaret. Watch out for grey seals, dolphins, sharks and occasionally whales.

Stage 6: Dysart to St Andrews

Beyond Dysart you reach Wemyss with its early Christian cave carvings (to which access is now restricted) and then the industrial ports of Leven-mouth, Buckhaven and Methil – the only one still operational. Proceeding by Largo you enter the East Neuk of Fife with its chain of harbours.

Earlsferry, now part of Elie, was the destination of the pilgrim ferry from North Berwick in East Lothian. St Monans has one of Scotland's oldest medieval par-ish churches. At Pittenweem, St Fillan's Cave is a modern shrine while the Priory, sited where the parish church now stands, was linked with the Celtic monas-tery of St Ethernan (later known as St Adrian) out on the Isle of May. Adrian and his fellow missionary

Monanus, after whom St Monans is named, were both killed on the island by Vikings following the defeat of the Scottish King Constantine II and his execution at Fife Ness. The boat to the island sails from the fishing town of Anstruther and arrives at Pilgrim Haven, where the well was believed to have properties of healing and fertility.

St Serf's mother, Thenew, sought refuge on the island when she was cast adrift and survived by drinking this precious fresh water. The island's name may mean Island of Maidens, suggesting an ancient place sacred to women. Later, with St Ethernan's legacy, the island was a major pilgrimage centre, and modern excavations have found many burials, including one of a pilgrim with the cockle shell of St James in his mouth.

Continuing through the beautiful East Neuk towards St Andrews, turn right off the main road at the sign for Dunino Church to encounter an exceptional combination of Pictish and Christian culture. Just beyond the church amid the trees is a hidden glen with a sacred pool formed from the natural rock and, a little further on, a rare set of rock carvings. You reach St Andrews on the southern harbour side, looking up to the site of the original monastic settlement on the headland. This has been a very Celtic journey, inspired by Scotland's medieval Queen and Saint, while passing through some of the most distinctively Scottish townscapes of later centuries. And always at your side is the sea with its brisk east winds and sharp clear light.

God be our star and harbour, God be our sail and
tower of light
God our island and our open sea, God our fare-
well and our arriving
God be our haven and our danger, God be our
storm and our still waters.

Stage 7: St Andrews

All routes, coastal and inland, merge in St Andrews,
centre of medieval and modern pilgrimage, and a
Celtic place of prayer. Columba and Andrew, Catholic Orthodox and Protestant conjoin, in a place where
religious conflict in the sixteenth and seventeenth
centuries claimed victims on all sides.

Each of the town's main thoroughfares points to
the Cathedral. Explore the life of medieval pilgrims
at St Andrews Museum. Visit the distinctive churches
of many traditions, including Holy Trinity Parish
Church in the centre where John Knox preached his
first sermon as a Protestant. The University retains its
medieval colleges, with St Salvator's notable chapel.
Then progress to the Cathedral with its ruined majesty and superb artefacts, including the St Andrews
Sarcophagus, a masterwork of Celtic Christian stone
carving, and the freestanding St Rule's Tower. The
relics of St Andrew, however, reputedly brought from
Greece by St Rule, were dispersed at the Reformation.

By pilgrim town and Cathedral ruin we come on
the headland to St Mary's Chapel by the sea, solitary

point of contemplation, and probably the site of the first Celtic monastery. They took literally the command to carry faith to the ends of the earth. On a cold clear night you can look out on never resting waves beneath a still starlit sky.

EVENING

Had I the heavens' embroidered cloths,
Enwrought with gold and silver light,
The blue and the dim and the dark cloths
Of night and light and the half-light,
I would spread the cloths under your feet:
But I, being poor, have only my dreams;
I have spread my dreams under your feet;
Tread softly because you tread on my dreams.
(*W. B. Yeats*)

BLESSING

Holy Gospel be your guide
Holy Gospel be your staff
Holy Gospel be companion on your way
For sweeter than honey
Richer than gold
Better than fame or glory
Are its holy pages to the lost,
The seeker and the listener,
Pearl of wisdom and
Bright jewel of heavenly love.

MIDWAY ON THE JOURNEY

You are before me and behind,
You search me and know me,
In my sitting down and standing up,
You understand my thoughts,
You keep my rest and my rising,
Upholding me in your hand.

Such knowledge is too wonderful for me,
Too high, too hard to understand.
Where can I go from your spirit?
If I climb into the heavens you are there,
If I descend below the earth I find you.
If I take the wings of the morning,
Or reach the furthest bounds of the sea,
Even there you meet me.

Surely the darkness will cover,
And night will be my shelter.
But darkness is not dark to you,
Night is radiant as day.
In the womb you shaped the mystery
Of who I am, my spirit knows
You as its own maker.
(*from Psalm 139*)

Route Eight
Tweed to Tyne:
The St Cuthbert
Pilgrim Journey

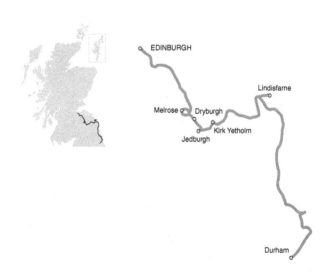

From Edinburgh to Melrose and Holy Island, you follow Cuthbert's quest for peace in a troubled age. You can also follow the St Cuthbert's Way, a signposted walking route from Melrose to Lindisfarne, and connect with Scotland's Borders Abbeys Way which maps out the routes between Jedburgh, Kelso, Dryburgh and Melrose Abbeys. The Pilgrim Journey continues to Cuthbert's final resting place at Durham.

Cuthbert is one of the most fully documented and most attractive of the early missionary saints. A vivid sense of a strong, gentle personality captured by an even stronger, gentler love of God comes through the places and the stories, many preserved by the Venerable Bede. First shepherd, then soldier, monk, reluctant bishop and hermit, Cuthbert's is a very human journey, though orientated towards the inner peace of God.

Cuthbert's story also unites the Celtic world and the Anglian or Northumbrian church, in the tradition of Columba and Aidan. On this journey you encounter quiet strength and peaceful meditation, amid natural repose.

MORNING

We know tension
between the world's pull
and inner space.
For Cuthbert it was people
to be cared for and guided,
alongside the call of sacred solitude –
the wild uninhabited places where nature
dwells undivided. Divine intimation,
welcome, unbidden.

BLESSING

From Iona to Lindisfarne
Aidan comes in faith and love,
From Lindisfarne to Melrose
Boisil comes in simple service,
From Channelkirk to Melrose
Cuthbert comes in hope and trust.
From Melrose to Dryburgh
Scott comes in search of beauty.
From Edinburgh to Dryburgh
To Melrose we come –
May open eyes and hearts
Be ours at every turning.

Stage 1: Edinburgh to Melrose

The journey begins below Edinburgh Castle on the site of Edinburgh's oldest church, St Cuthbert's. Here the gentle Saint of Lothian and Northumbria is celebrated with contemporary devotion. We follow his life story by following the Roman route south to Dalkeith and Eskbank, from which you can divert to Newbattle Abbey where the much later Cistercians of Melrose founded a sister house in a similar situation by a wooded riverside.

South of Gorebridge, we cut across by the medieval churches of Borthwick and Crichton, associated with Kentigern and each linked to a substantial castle, to rejoin the Roman road, which Cuthbert used frequently on his missionary and pastoral journeys. The modern road, though, veers off course, and to find the original orientation divert again briefly to Soutra Aisle, where little remains of a major medieval hospital. The road then continued by Kirkton of Channelkirk where Cuthbert possibly spent his childhood. This wild hill country shows why in his youth Cuthbert was known as a shepherd and a soldier.

But spiritual dreams and longings took the young Cuthbert south. After Lauder and Earlston, Scott's View on the hill road looks down directly on to Old Melrose. Cuthbert came to the monastery, founded by St Aidan in this bend of the river, just after the missionary from Iona had died on Lindisfarne. As the monks stood shocked by the news, the young soldier galloped up and made straight for the church. The wise and kindly Prior Boisil immediately saw that the future had arrived. Cuthbert was received into the monastery, beginning at the bottom with the humblest tasks and service. Our journey continues by way of beautiful Dryburgh and St Boswell's, named for Boisil, round the Eildon Hills to Melrose.

Stage 2: Melrose to Jedburgh

We begin from the Cistercian Abbey of Melrose, beside the town. It has its own Abbot Saint – Waltheof – and its own rich heritage, including the heart of Robert the Bruce. The discovery of the heart's resting place was a consolation after it failed to reach Jerusalem on a crusade that was Bruce's dying wish. We follow Cuthbert on his journey from Old Melrose downriver to become Prior of Lindisfarne. You can walk this route on St Cuthbert's Way via the Eildons, or use a variety of transport via Old Melrose, Newstead and St Boswell's, touching Dryburgh again by bridge from the near side of the Tweed.

Roman remains coincide on this route with the old British Christianity of saints like Mungo, Ninian and Modan, who may have founded the first place of retreat at Dryburgh. South of Dryburgh, there are medieval churches associated with Boisil. While St Cuthbert's Way turns east, we continue to Jedburgh with its magnificent ruined Abbey.

St Margaret's son, King David, is the moving spirit behind the great Border Abbeys at Melrose, Kelso, Dryburgh and Jedburgh. When the fortunes of Scotland's Catholic rulers declined under English pressure in the reign of Mary Queen of Scots, these huge complexes began their career as romantic ruins. A circular Borders Abbey Way takes in all the resonant locations.

These, however, are not Cuthbert's personal places. His instinct is for the hills and valleys and, ultimately, for remote rocky islands. So we resume in his footsteps. During Cuthbert's last months at Old Melrose, Boisil, who knew he was dying of the plague, read to Cuthbert from a Commentary on John's Gospel. This deeply mystical inspiration, combined with a very practical mindset, was to guide the younger man throughout his life. Cuthbert was buried with a copy of John's Gospel by his side.

Door of the sheepfold, Water of the Well of Life,
True Bread that satisfies all hunger, True Word that nourishes the heart,
May we follow the mystery of Cuthbert's faith and passion,
Where he placed his footsteps, in the way of the Good Shepherd.

ON THE WAY

CUDDY'S CHICKENS

Cuddy's Chickens' is the nickname which people in Northumberland still give to the eider ducks which Saint Cuthbert – Cuddy – knew and loved.

Cuthbert was brought up near Melrose in the Scottish Borders, where he was a shepherd and well known as a champion wrestler. Even then he was a gentle giant of a man, who often felt close to God when he was alone in the hills with his sheep. Then Cuthbert became a monk in the monastery at Melrose and later he went to look after the community of monks which had been started on the Island of Lindisfarne off the coast of Northumberland.

Although Cuthbert worked hard, telling the country people about God's love and trying to help everyone, he also liked sometimes to be alone with God. So Cuthbert built himself a place of refuge or retreat on the Fame Islands off Lindisfarne. These places were often known as 'Dysarts' or 'Deserts' after the holy men and women who had gone to the desert in Egypt to pray. But the 'Dysart' on the Farne Islands was all rocks, sea and wind, not sand and sun!

First, Cuthbert built himself a low thick wall in a stone circle open to the sky. Inside the circle he

built a little prayer hut for himself and a small
hut for guests. They were both made of rough
boulders with a thatched roof. Inside the stone
circle there was also a little spring well of fresh
water and in the shelter of the wall Cuthbert
grew some corn and a few vegetables to eat.
Lots of birds come to the Farne Islands, and
Cuthbert got to know them well. The ravens
came and ate his corn, and the eider ducks
came across to visit. There were seagulls and
fulmars, kittiwakes and puffins. Cuthbert loved
them all. The seals came to fish and to lie on the
rocks when it was sunny, and far out to sea the
dolphins and the whales swam by.
Often Cuthbert would stay up late praying
to God that people would have strength to
change all the terrible and wicked things
that were happening in the world – wars and
famines, murder, torture and cruelty. One night
when Cuthbert was on his knees on the shore
praying, he allowed the cold salt water to wash
round him. What was the cold compared to
the bitter things Jesus had suffered for men and
women?
When he came out of the sea Cuthbert was
so stiff and frozen he could hardly move. Two
otters slipped out of the water and going up
to Cuthbert they rubbed his legs and feet with
their warm, waterproof bodies. Gentle Cuthbert
kept very still until the otters slipped back into

the sea. Then he found he was able to stand up and move freely. So perhaps the otters in Northumberland should be called 'Cuddy's slippers'?

THE EAGLE AND THE FISH

One time Cuthbert was travelling round, calling at different villages. He had a young boy with him, and they were both tired out.
'Where will we eat tonight?' asked Cuthbert.
'I don't know', said the boy. 'We haven't brought any food with us and we won't reach the next village till tomorrow.'
'Do you see that bird up there?' said Cuthbert. The boy looked up and saw an eagle high overhead. 'God could send us some food by that eagle', Cuthbert continued.
So they walked along a river, chatting to each other about the animals and birds they had seen. Suddenly they saw the eagle land on the bank of the river.
'Quick', said Cuthbert, 'run and see what the eagle has brought'.
The boy came back with a huge fish which the eagle had caught and dropped from its talons.
'Cut the fish in two', said Cuthbert, 'and give the eagle back half'.
Then Cuthbert built a small fire and they cooked their half of the fish for supper.

BLESSING

May the blessing
Of all created things,
Harvest of the land,
Savour of the sea,
Salmon running in the river,
Birds wheeling in the air,
And all that tends life,
Sowing of the grain,
Making of bread,
Nurture of souls,
Be yours, in the spirit and
In the peace of Cuthbert.

Stage 3: Jedburgh to Lindisfarne

By Morebattle, Linton and Yetholm, we travel through
Cuthbert's country parish. Here he visited and nursed,
shared the sacraments, taught and encouraged. One
of the most touching of Cuthbert's relics is the little
portable altar, later ornamented with silver, which
became the focus of loving community wherever he
went. The ancient churches in these Cheviot villages
are the legacy of his labour as a healer and shepherd
of souls.

Just past Kirk Yetholm is the site of the Chapel
St Ethelreda, the reluctant Queen whose flight took
her to St Abb's Head and finally to Ely where she
founded the monastery which became the Cathedral

of the Fens. This valley of the Glen was a power-house of British Christianity. At Kirknewton, the medieval Church of St Gregory remembers the sending of St Augustine to Canterbury in 597, the year of Columba's death on Iona. Just beyond the village at Gefrin, below the hill fortress of Yeavering Bell, St Paulinus, a forerunner of Pope Gregory's mission, conducted mass baptisms in the river. A monument and walkway marks what was once an important royal centre. At Kirknewton, the female tradition of Northumbrian Christianity continues with commemoration of Josephine Butler, whose campaigning work on behalf of prostitutes exposed the hypocrisies of a later supposedly Christian society.

But the predominant influence here today is still Cuthbert's, as we continue by Wooler towards the coast. St Cuthbert's Cave is a natural retreat, and, though the origins of the site are obscure, it has been adopted because it is so redolent of the authentic Cuthbert spirit. One of the defining moments of the journey is to climb the rise beyond the Cave to see the ocean, islands and shores rolled out beneath.

There is the Holy Island of Aidan and Cuthbert, with the rocky retreats of St Cuthbert's Isle and the Inner Farne. The Prior's journey was ever towards greater prayerful solitude, till, as a reluctant Bishop, he was drawn back into mission and pastoral care. Though his heartfelt wish to die on his Farne Hermitage was granted, Cuthbert's body was brought back to Lindisfarne to become an object of pilgrimage and devotion.

Stage 4: Lindisfarne to Durham

Lindisfarne, with the Priory ruins and thriving pilgrim Church of St Mary, is a highpoint but not a conclusion. From here the heritage ripples out, and even the destruction of the Priory by Norse raiders only served to spread Cuthbert's influence. The subsequent wanderings of the saint's body covered the whole of northern England, ending finally at Durham, where the massive Cathedral owes its origins to the humble shepherd pastor.

But at Bamburgh, Newcastle, Tynemouth, Jarrow and Wearmouth, we encounter not just the influence of the saint but a wave of culture and Christian civilisation. Whether in the pages of the Lindisfarne Gospels, the lucent writings of the Venerable Bede, Anglo Saxon carving, or the ecstatic visionary poetry of Caedmon, we are bathed in a light of spiritual inspiration. Moreover, the harmonious presence of Celtic patterns in this artistic upsurge belies the idea that divisions about the dating of Easter are the main story. In St Peter's at Bamburgh, on Inner Farne, or at Durham itself, you realise that St Aidan and St Cuthbert are in unbroken communion, undisturbed by Synods of Whitby, or supposed doctrinal divisions.

At Durham, the final destination, you can still visit Cuthbert's shrine and see the precious cross, Gospel of John, and portable altar which were placed in his coffin. Though his devoted labour was in Jarrow, Bede was also later moved here, his bones united with Cuthbert's. This is appropriate since it is through his graceful storytelling that we know so much about Cuthbert.

EVENING

We pray you, noble Jesu,
That as you have graciously
Granted us joyfully to imbibe
The words of your knowledge,
So you will also grant us
To come at last to yourself,
Fount of all wisdom,
To dwell in your presence
Forever.
(*Prayer of Bede*)

BLESSING

Let a Trinity of light,
wisdom, love and learning,
three candles on the altar
lit by the Holy Spirit,
shining through centuries
of doubt and trouble,
illumine our darkness.
Christ is the morning star
who, when the night is past,
brings the light of life
and opens everlasting day.

Route Nine
Lothian and Lammermuir:
The St Bea and St Baldred
Pilgrim Journey

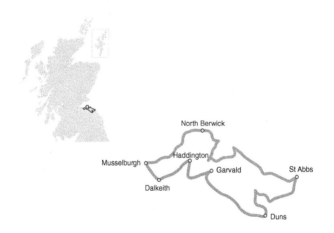

Neither Bea nor Baldred can be described as household names. But that is exactly what makes this Pilgrim Journey so revealing. East Lothian and Berwickshire form a very distinctive area of Scotland with its own culture, history and spiritual traditions, as well as its own landscape, seascape and an unrivalled cluster of historic towns and villages.

The story of the region is closely bound up with its successive historical waves. Early Celtic culture, including seaborne Irish influence, was succeeded by Anglo-Saxon and Norman-Scottish eras, all connected with northern England as much as with the rest of Scotland. In Christian terms the early Celtic missionaries, including Aidan of Lindisfarne and Cuthbert of Melrose, birthed a Northumbrian Church that in turn brought a unique blend of Celtic and Saxon Christianity to the area. This forms a major part of its special heritage, unique in Scotland though also prevalent in Northumbria.

But there is something more – elusive perhaps but definite. Land and sea seem to match one to the other in vivid definition and clear light. The Lammermuir range traverses the long Firth of Forth, or is it the other way round? The level expanses are waymarked by the very definite contours of Arthur's Seat, North Berwick Law, Traprain Law and the Bass Rock. Further out in the mouth of the estuary sits the rocky Isle of May, like a dream isle of the deep that seems at times to float on the horizon. The quality of light is in and through everything, with subtle and ever-shifting changes of perception. It is a sacred landscape that draws artists, naturalists, scientists, poets and visionaries to its contemplation.

Last but not least, East Lothian and Berwickshire have more female than male saints in their accumulated traditions. That is intriguing since, compared to some other regions of Scotland, the landscape could be described as masculine in its rocky definitions. Which only goes to prove that conventional gender categories are not part of the early Christian story, especially on this Journey.

MORNING

Light on the river may be grey, white waved,
Blue sun dancing, or shining smooth like glass.
Watch the skies move in cloud and bright breeze,
As we take the road between the widening sea
And the long ridgeways, Moorfoot and
Lammermuir.
How far we see, living between the two natures,
A land formed by both, and the heavens beyond.

BLESSING

May this day be a new journey
The beginning of something fresh,
Softly or sharply focussed, and surprising.
And if we have travelled this way before
May the road rise to meet us as a friend.

Stage 1: Musselburgh to North Berwick

The 'honest toun' of Musselburgh is a very old Scottish burgh, but its parish church of St Michael's, sited on a slight hill at Inveresk a little to the south, takes us beyond old into ancient. This was a major Roman fortress looking down on the Roman bridge over the Esk. This conjunction of Roman settlement with an early Christian church, repeated at Cramond on the west side of Edinburgh, is a reminder that Christianity first reached Scotland because it was spreading to the furthest outposts of the Roman Empire.

On the east side of Musselburgh near the race-course is Loretto School, sited at Pinkie House, the former mansion of the Earls of Dunfermline. But Loretto was originally a burgeoning centre of late medieval pilgrimage. The hermit of Loretto was a major attraction, living beside a replica of the house of Mary, Mother of God, in Nazareth, which had been miraculously transported from Palestine to Loretto in Italy. The huge popularity of this devotion is a reminder that the medieval Scottish Church was far from moribund as the Protestant Reformation took hold. In 1536 James V walked barefoot from Edinburgh to Loretto. At the same time shrines like Loretto were specifically targeted as examples of 'superstition', which was opposed to 'true faith' by the radical Protestants, who were often concentrated in trading towns like Musselburgh.

Prestonpans, Cockenzie and Port Seton stretch out along the shore, each with their own seagoing traditions, local industries and distinctive churches. Beyond Port Seton, the journey becomes more rural with coastal villages and churches that retain a six-teenth- or seventeenth-century character. Aberlady is reputedly where Thenew, Tennoch or Enoch, mother of St Kentigern, was cast adrift by her irate father, Loth. But the fish, seals and dolphins departed with her, never to return. Perhaps that is why the village is now best known as a bird sanctuary.

In the wood between Aberlady and Luffness are to be found the simple remains of a Carmelite Friary complete with a knight's tomb. At Gullane, the medi-eval church was abandoned due to sandstorms and replaced by the parish kirk at Dirleton, which is one of Scotland's finest early post-reformation buildings. Even the little island of Fidra, off the beach north of Dirleton, has the ruins of a medieval chapel of St Nicolas.

North Berwick was a pilgrim hub, feeding the faithful by boat over to St Andrews. But in addi-tion to its pilgrim chapel at the harbour – now a ruin – North Berwick contains its own ancient Celtic chapel on the Law, an important medieval parish church with its modern successors, a ruined Cistercian convent, and a Seabird Centre. From North Berwick you look out onto the austere open waters of the firth, with the rocky retreat of the Bass inshore. Here in this exposed spot St Baldred had his chapel where, later, devoted Covenanters were imprisoned. Further out is the Isle of May with its grey seals and sacred well, where the Irish saints Adrian or Ethernan and Monanus were martyred. The cumulative weight of history leans heavily, yet this bright seaside town has an almost French atmosphere, bathed in a companionable light that only turns austere out on the open waves in a grey light.

Stage 2: North Berwick to Coldingham

By land and sea, North Berwick is the doorway to the heartland of Baldred, Scotland's Anglo-Saxon saint. Baldred founded churches at Auldhame, Whitekirk, and Prestonkirk, along with a monastery at Tyningham, and a cave retreat at Seacliff beach beyond Auldhame, in addition to the Bass Rock chapel. The rock formation off the point at Tyningham is still called St Baldred's Cradle. St Baldred's Boat is another coastal feature by Tantallon Castle. Only some of this achievement is still visible. The medieval church in the grounds of Tyningham House may be the site of Baldred's monastery, while Prestonkirk, probably the saint's burial place, is built on a very ancient mound with Baldred's well still flowing by the riverside below.

Archaeology has revealed the extent of the Auldhame settlement, but there is little to see above ground. Whitekirk, on the road south from Auldhame, later developed as an important Marian shrine. Sadly, the healing well was covered over but the medieval church and a tithe barn, which marks the site of the pilgrim hostels, remain. Suffragettes set fire to the church in 1914 because of connections between the Conservative leader A.J. Balfour and local landed families.

From East Linton we proceed to Traprain Law where a sizable early Celtic town was located. This is the birthplace of Thenew, Mungo's mother, and the scene of her trials at the hand of her father Loth, King of the British, Celtic Gododdin. At Standingstane Farm, Loth's stone looks defiantly towards the cliff over which, on learning she was pregnant, he had Thenew thrown in a ritual chariot. But she survived unharmed. We go back towards Stenton, paying our respects at the Rood Well on the far side of the village and then approach Dunbar through Spott which has a medieval church, once a first pilgrim station on the long trek westwards to Iona.

Dunbar was the headquarters of Bea or Bega, an Irish Christian who worked with Hilda of Whitby. Her church was on the site of the present impressive parish kirk but, in general, Dunbar has the character of a scenic harbour town, in which the older remains of castle and church have succumbed to sea and wind. John Muir, the world famous environmentalist and founder of the national park movement, was born here in a main-street house which is now an interpretative centre. Continuing along the coast, we reach the village of Cockburnspath with its linked harbour at Cove. Beyond Cove a left turn off the main road goes to Pease Bay where St Helen's church is sited above the sands. This is the last potential stop before reaching Coldingham and St Abbs.

ON THE WAY

St Abbs upon the Nabbs
St Helens upon the Lea
St Beas upon Dunbar sands
Stands closest to the sea.

HARDY AND DETERMINED WOMEN

Christian story is full of vivid female lives from the women disciples in the New Testament, through the stories of the saints, to the present day. East Lothian and Berwickshire's Christian saga begins with the remarkable Tennoch or Thenew, who survives rape, ritual execution and abandonment to give birth on a beach and ensure the next chapter of Scotland's history.

After Thenew comes a group of Anglo-Saxon women including Hilda, Ebbe, Bea and Helen, who take the lead in Christian affairs, founding monasteries and churches, commanding men and women alike. This heritage inspires Marian devotion through sacred wells, through pilgrimages and through churches and monasteries dedicated to St Mary the Virgin.

So the reaction and repression, when it comes in this area, is all the more violent with witch trials, executions, the stopping of wells, the banning of pilgrimages and the imposition of a male-dominated mercantile culture.

For all his radical virtues, John Knox, a child of Haddington, had little conception of gender equality, far less of the leadership of women. Perhaps the future of the Church lies once more today in the hands, minds and hearts of women. None too soon. It would be good if St Mary's Well at Whitekirk could be opened up for a new millennium, as it is still there in its original site waiting to flow.

BLESSING

May we find the hidden streams
Release the forgotten wells,
Drinking deep and long from the waters
Of the well of life, springing inside us.

Stage 3: St Abbs to Nunraw
By Duns and Abbey St Bathans

The parish church of Coldingham preserves the choir of the medieval Priory church which stood on this site. But this lovely medieval settlement replaced a more austere early community on the headlands of

St Abbs. That exposed site, of which no visible signs remain, was moved after the Viking onslaught, and the area is now a nature reserve commanding spectacular cliffs and extensive seabird colonies.

But we do still have the story of St Ebbe, an Anglo-Saxon princess who, along with her sister Hilda, fell under the influence of the Columban church on Lindisfarne. Ebbe established her own monastery on the cliffs at St Abbs, where there may once have been a Roman fort. It was a favourite stopping place for Cuthbert, who is described as going down to the shore to pray at night with the cold waves lapping round his legs. A young monk watched two otters coming out of the sea to rub the absentminded saint's limbs and restore the blood flow. Ebbe's community was for men and women, and later attracted criticism from the prurient.

The village of St Abb's is a short walk from the Nature Reserve Visitor Centre. In addition to the attractive harbour there is a St Ebbe Centre and an Information hub with interpretation of the local environment. It is also worth going on into Eyemouth, which is Berwickshire's main fishing port and a present-day hub of sea life and leisure. Our route however turns back to Coldingham then on to Reston, Bonkyl Church, Preston and Duns. Once the county town, Duns is a quiet place that nonetheless produced Scotland greatest ever theologian, the medieval Franciscan scholar Duns Scotus, who carved out his radical intellectual path at Oxford and Paris and was later canonised.

From Duns the journey takes to the Lammermuirs which have been constantly in our range of vision from the coastal route. The lonely roads wend through moors, past reservoirs and across river valleys. You can divert north to see Abbey St Bathans where the church is on the site of a medieval nunnery that may have replaced a Celtic religious settlement associated with the Edenhall broch and fort on the hill above. There was, however, no St Bathan or Bothon, which is a term for peasant houses. To the north is the old village of Longformacus with its fine little medieval church, now sadly closed. Both places are on the Southern Upland Way. We follow the Whiteadder river north-east to Nunraw and Garvald.

Stage 4: Garvald to Musselburgh By Haddington

Coming down towards Nunraw, we pass the kind of hill settlement where Thenew or Tennoch was sent as a young woman in disgrace to tend the sheep and pigs. Next comes the farm at Grange of Nunraw, which belonged in medieval times to the Cistercian nunnery in Haddington. In 1946 Cistercian monks came here to build the first new Cistercian community in Scotland since the Reformation. The monastery chapel can be visited at any time. The outlook from here to Traprain Law and the East Lothian coast is superb. Don't miss the memorial garden beside the cemetery, which is dedicated to the Cistercian monks who were victims of the civil war in Algeria.

From Garvald village at the foot of the hill, we proceed further along the Lammermuir edge to Gifford. The village is headed by the handsome Yester Kirk, which replaced the fine medieval Bathans Church, now located in the grounds of Yester House at the other end of the village. The Hays of Yester cleared the original village to Gifford in order to create a private landscaped park. Rev John Witherspoon, the republican, Presbyterian champion of American independence, came from Gifford and has a memorial at the newer building. Perhaps the landlordism of his home village contributed to his later radicalism.

The main road out of Gifford goes by Bolton and Lennoxlove to Haddington. One of Scotland's finest medieval burghs, Haddington contained an array of chapels and religious foundations. The original 'Lamp of the Lothian' was a Franciscan Friary located near the lovely present-day Episcopal Church of the Holy Trinity. The Cistercian Convent was on the east bank of the Tyne, and later incorporated St Martin's Church, a very old foundation which is still a standing ruin. But the main surviving glory of Haddington is the substantial St Mary's Town Kirk, which outsizes many abbeys and cathedrals. There are many interesting details including the ecumenical Chapel of the Three Kings, and an exhibition about the sixteenth-century siege of Haddington.

Complete the journey by way of the medieval church and village of Pencaitland, back to Musselburgh – the Honest Toun.

EVENING

Returning home, journey done, past
Low lying fields aglow with last
West rays folding into twilight.
Winter, summer, autumn, spring,
Everything revolves in season,
Giving every day its reason.
New lights blink out along the firth
Houses of light, hospitable fires,
Lamps of Lothian shine through the night.

BLESSING

At the closing of the day
Gather up the moments,
Holding the time together
Precious before sleep.
And may rest be on our eyes
Peace of journey done,
Hope for each new dawn.

Route Ten
From Coast to Coast:
The St Andrew
Pilgrim Journey

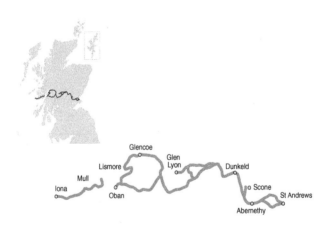

From Iona to St Andrews, or St Andrews to Iona, you follow the birth of Scotland through its major pilgrim shrines. By way of Iona, Dunkeld, Scone, Abernethy and St Andrews, an emergent nation fashioned its spiritual identity. This required a blending of different Celtic traditions – Irish, Pictish and British – and a continual interaction with the European mainland.

Many external pressures, not least Viking incursions from the north and English territorial ambitions from the south, led the different regional peoples of what we now call Scotland to fashion a nation. Christianity was central to this process in ways that still resonate in cultural and political life.

There is history aplenty on this journey but also exceptional scenic variety and beauty. From the Inner Hebrides, through Argyllshire, Highland Perthshire and into Tayside you experience a dimension of Scotland that is Highland and Lowland, with settled valleys and wooded glens alongside the familiar mountains. Attractive towns and villages are on all sides with many historic churches nestling in their midst.

The route also links twenty first-century sanctuaries that nurture a modern sense of peace and self-discovery. Iona and St Andrews are contrasting centres of international attention, while Dunkeld sits quietly by the Tay in winsome wooded retreat.

MORNING

Iona, Columba
Dove of the Church
Sign of Peace
Native to the Light
Light to the Stranger
Native to the Land
If you have love one to another
Love unfeigned, a heart sincere,
Then God the helper of all things good.
Will strengthen and comfort you.
(*St Columba*)

BLESSING

The Guiding of Columba
be on your going and returning
in strath and on ridge
through pit and mire
over hill and crag.
The peace of God be your portion
and let light perpetual
shine upon you.

Stage 1: Iona

Iona is Columba's Isle, though it was a sacred place before he arrived. The restored Benedictine Abbey should be experienced as part of the whole island with its many places of peace and beauty, including the ruined nunnery and the ancient burial ground of Scotland's kings at St Oran's Chapel. Martyr's Bay, where Viking raiders slaughtered the later monks, and Columba's Bay, which was the Saint's own landfall, are also evocative of the island's special atmosphere and story.

The people of Iona have their own community identity which can be explored through visits to the parish church and nearby heritage centre. But the presence of Columba, even after more than fourteen hundred years, continues to imbue every aspect of the island. This was prophesied by Columba himself in the last few days of his life in 597, as recorded by Adomnan:

This place however small and lowly, will have bestowed on it no small but great honour by the kings and peoples, and also by the rulers of even barbarous and foreign nations with their subject tribes. And the Saints of other churches too will give it great reverence.

The restoration first of the Abbey Church and then, through the leadership of the twentieth-century Iona Community, the Abbey buildings, is one of Scottish

Christianity's resurrection stories that continues to resonate internationally. Again, Gaelic tradition, of which Columba himself was such a notable champion, foresaw this development.

> Iona of my heart, Iona of my love,
> Instead of monks' voices will be the lowing of cattle;
> But ere the world will come to an end
> Iona shall be as it was.

Stage 2: Oban to Tyndrum

From Iona to Oban you traverse the lovely yet austere Ross of Mull, cross the south of the island, and make a beautiful sea crossing past the islands of Lismore and Kerrera, which were both the homes of Celtic monasteries.

Oban is a West Highland capital with two Cathedrals and other lovely churches. It is also a gateway to Argyll with its lochs, villages, castles and mountains. Going inland by Dunollie Castle, you turn at Dalmally into Glenorchy. These rolling straths with their mountainous terrain were once known as the refuge, or retreat, of the hermits. Like the Desert Fathers, Celtic saints sought God in the wild places. Glenorchy is a beautiful quiet valley leading towards higher hill country with its wide, silent spaces. At Bridge of Orchy you join the main road south to Tyndrum.

By an alternative northern loop to Tyndrum, you visit the islands and lochs of the Celtic apostles, where they found places of refuge and refreshing. By Ardchattan and Lismore – which was the great sanctuary of St Moluag – and Eilean Munde in Loch Leven, burial place of Fintan Munnu, you tread the boundary of sea and land.

Lismore is a short boat trip from Port Appin. The ancient church, once a cathedral of St Moluag, is two miles north of the pier at Clachan. Also buried there is Alexander Cramichael whose collection of Gaelic prayers and blessings sparked a Celtic revival across the globe. The inscription on his gravestone reads, 'Be my soul in peace with the brightness of the mountains. Valiant Michael, meet thou my soul.'

Back on the mainland, in dramatic Glencoe you can visit the village and, beyond, a memorial to the massacre. Recall with sorrow the bloodshed when politics and religion clash. This too is part of Scotland's faith story, which we see reflected in the contemporary world. The National Trust Visitor Centre on the other side of the road celebrates the unique ecology of Glencoe and not just its sad history.

Moluag, the clear, the brilliant Sun of Lismore,
Great Garden, Sanctuary, Enclosure,
May light divine shine from you,
And the God of love ward off evil and violence
From the people of Alba, and all earth's children.

Stage 3: Tyndrum to Aberfeldy

Follow St Fillan, by travelling from Lochalsh to Tyndrum and then eastwards through Glen Dochart. On the way, he left healing places associated with sources of natural water, and sacred relics which played a special part in Scotland's story. These include Fillan's hand-bell and staff or crozier, which are now in the National Museum of Scotland in Edinburgh, and the Saint's arm-bone – now lost – which was carried into battle at Bannockburn. Robert the Bruce was ever after a devotee of St Fillan, committing his relics to the care of their hereditary guardians, the Dewars.

At Strathfillan Church on the main road, by walking a short distance on the West Highland Way, you find the remains of St Fillan's medieval Priory with its ancient font. A little downriver you can also visit the Holy Pool, where people went for healing, possibly the site of St Fillan's original settlement. This is a peaceful, almost neglected spot, that has a special place in the story of Scottish pilgrimage.

At the Visitor Information centre in the old mill at Killin, you can follow the whole saga of Fillan, and see the healing stones associated with his ancient cures. In living water, still and flowing, we touch sources close to elemental life and divine creation.

St Fillan's influence takes you on by Lochearnhead and Comrie into the heart of Perthshire, but our route continues by Loch Tay to Aberfeldy.

Stage 4: Glen Lyon Loop

On this additional loop, we follow St Adomnan, Abbot of Iona, through Argyll and into the Perthshire glens, pausing at ancient places of Christian story. Walkers can trace Adomnan's actual steps from Bridge of Orchy over the pass by Ben Doran into Glen Lyon. By road past Killin, you can climb steeply on the west side of Ben Lawers into the glen, or continue to Kenmore and go into the mouth of the glen. The minor road from Kenmore on the north side of the Tay takes you by Inchadrey, which is the original church site. James MacGregor, the Dean of Lismore and earliest compiler of the older Gaelic poetry, is buried here.

Adomnan was the biographer of Columba, author of a guide to the pilgrim sites of the Holy Land, and deviser of a law to protect non-combatants in war. He has left his mark on many sites in Glenlyon including Fortingall, with its ancient yew, where he founded a monastery at an ancient druidic site. His traditional burial place is at Dull, where the sanctuary garth survived for many centuries. Its boundary crosses are at Dull and at Weem. His hand-bell is preserved at Innerwick near Bridge of Balgie, and his font at Fortingall.

In Strath Appin, between Glenlyon and Aberfeldy, southern saints also came on Highland retreat, including St Cuthbert at Dull, and St Cedd, the Saxon missionary. He and his brother St Chad, remembered at Foss, were associated with Lindisfarne. One can imagine the attractions of this wooded Perthshire glen in comparison with the open skies and sea spray of Lindisfarne.

ON THE WAY

The Lord is my shepherd
I shall not want
He makes me to lie down in green pastures
He leads me beside quiet waters,
He restores my soul.
He guides me in the paths of righteousness
For His name's sake
Even though I walk
Through the valley of the shadow of death
I will fear no evil
For you are with me,
Your rod and your staff they comfort me.
(*from Psalm 23*)

THE SHEILINGS

Between the Festival of Beltane at the beginning of May and autumn time, many Highlanders moved into temporary shelters in the upper glens. There they herded their cattle, made cheese, and took full advantage of the summer

months, while the crops grew on the lower
ground.

The sheilings were places of happiness, laughter,
dancing and song, according to the older
poems. In Glen Cailleach on this walking route,
above Glen Lyon, you can visit the symbolic
sheiling of the Celtic divinities, the Cailleach
and the Bodach, and their children. According
to custom, they are taken out of their shelter at
Beltane and then returned inside for the winter
season.

The coming of Christianity did not change all
the old ways; in fact the appeal of Christianity
to many was its strengthening and deepening
of ancient beliefs about creation and a spiritual
realm. The early saints also sought the upper
glens as places of contemplation and renewal.

BLESSING

O Son of the living God,
Ancient ruler of days,
My desire is a hut hidden in the wilderness –
Making it my home –
A narrow blue stream beside,
And a clear pool for the washing
Away of sin by grace of the Holy Spirit,
Surrounded by lovely trees nursing
The birds with their different voices

Sheltering them with green foliage,
Looking south for warmth, watered
Well for plants of every sort to grow.
A beautiful chapel hung with veils
A home for God from heaven
And bright lamps above the white gospels.
Enough of food and clothing to live
Sitting for a time and meditating
On God in every place.

Stage 5: Aberfeldy and Glenlyon to Dunkeld and Scone

Scotland's ancient kingdom was formed around these places. Picts and Scots were symbolically united by moving Columba's relics at Dunkeld, after the Viking onslaught on Iona. We have followed the spread of Scots influence with Adomnan through Glenlyon. The journey to Dunkeld traverses a landscape saturated with the legends of Finn and Ossian, which are celebrated at the Hermitage in Strathbraan. Dunkeld Cathedral sits in a beautiful bend of the River Tay amid gracious parks and woodland. It seems perfectly in place and its scale reminds us of its importance as the capital of Christianity in the southern Highlands. The attractive village spills down from the former Cathedral Close to the bridge over the Tay. Birnam, a little downriver, is also very attractive and associated with Shakespeare's Macbeth ('Till Birnam

Wood will come to Dunsinane') and Beatrix Potter, creator of Peter Rabbit.

At the Mound or Moot of Scone, the Kings of Scots were inaugurated upon the Stone of Destiny, which was reputed to have been Jacob's pillow, coming from Palestine to Argyll by way of Ireland, and finally to Scone when the Picts and Scots united. The Abbey here was ransacked during the Scottish Reformation, and absorbed into the aristocratic estate of what is now called Scone Palace.

The remains of Scone Abbey are in the grounds of Scone Palace, but the plain stone reputed to be the ancient coronation stone is in Edinburgh Castle, having been returned after a seven-hundred-year sojourn under the coronation chair in Westminster Abbey in London. Some say that the original stone is still buried where the monks concealed it in Perthshire, as Edward I's troops came to seize Scotland's precious symbol of nationhood.

Stage 6: Scone to St Andrews

Crossing the Tay and travelling the last leg to St Andrews you follow the path of kings, queens, hermits, and thousands of ordinary people through the medieval centuries. The monastic round tower at Abernethy points your way. There was a very old Celtic monastery here dedicated to St Brigid, and perhaps founded by members of her community. Sacred legend retains a priestess tradition in the

Abernethy story of St Donald and his nine saintly daughters, echoing even older Pictish lore of the nine maidens. There is an excellent local museum adjacent to the present churchyard, which is also the site of the monastery.

A direct route takes you by the market town of Cupar and its historic churches. Alternatively, staying close to the river by Newburgh you visit the peaceful monastery ruins of Balmerino. There are few areas of Scotland which retain so much of their medieval character as north-east Fife with its rich farmland surrounding prosperous villages and towns. On this leg the Tay broadens out into a sparkling sandy estuary to meet the bracing North Sea. The contrast with the tree-sheltered river banks at Dunkeld could not be greater.

By Leuchars and Guardbridge, you see your destination – a cluster of towers and spires where Scotland meets Europe by the salt-crested sea. Pilgrims, ancient and modern, are drawn to this spot where rock abuts the ocean, and time meets eternity.

Stage 7: St Andrews

All roads merge in St Andrews, centre of medieval and modern pilgrimage, at a Celtic place of prayer. Columba and Andrew, Catholic, Orthodox and Protestant conjoin, in a place where religious conflict in the sixteenth and seventeenth centuries claimed victims on all sides.

Each of the town's main thoroughfares points to the Cathedral. Explore the life of medieval pilgrims at St Andrews Museum. Visit the distinctive churches of many traditions, including Holy Trinity Parish Church in the centre where John Knox preached his first sermon as a Protestant. The University retains its medieval colleges, with St Salvator's notable chapel. Then progress to the Cathedral with its ruined majesty and superb artefacts, including the St Andrews Sarcophagus, a masterwork of Celtic Christian stone carving, and the freestanding St Rule's Tower. The relics of St Andrew, however, reputedly brought from Greece by St Rule, were dispersed at the Reformation.

By pilgrim town and Cathedral ruin we come finally to St Mary's Chapel by the sea, solitary point of contemplation, and probably the site of the first Celtic monastery. They took literally the command to carry faith to the ends of the earth. But what grew eventually here was not simple monastic cell but a consciously crafted Scottish Jerusalem.

EVENING

Bless God, all you servants of God
Who wait at night in the House of the Lord.
Lift up your hands in the holy place
And bless God.
God who made heaven and earth
Will bless you from Mount Sion.
(*Psalm 134*)

BLESSING

Let all Travellers and Pilgrims
Praise you
Let all the Apostles
Praise you
Let Mary Mother of God
Praise you
Let Saints and Martyrs
Praise you
Let the blessed departed
Praise you
Let we in our time and place
Praise you
Let this night and the darkness
Praise you
May this holy place
Be our sanctuary and guiding light,
Through all the ages.

Route Eleven
Angus Coast and Glens:
A Pictish Saints'
Pilgrim Journey

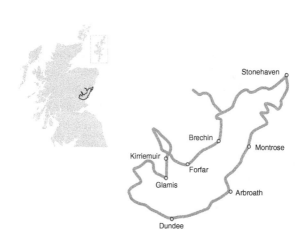

This Journey embraces Angus and what was formerly Kincardineshire – more popularly the Mearns. Though we have referred frequently to 'Picts' and 'Pictish' throughout northern and eastern Scotland, Angus and the Mearns contain an unparalleled concentration of Pictish monuments and remains, in particular the justly celebrated carved slabs and crosses. The Picts were a Celtic people long settled in these parts of Scotland, mixing with earlier peoples, and speaking a version of P-Celtic which also developed into Welsh and Breton. The mystery element arises because after the union of the Picts and Scots, the Pictish language lost out to the greater prestige of the Irish-Scots Gaelic tradition, and never made the grade as a written tongue, so disappearing.

But on the ground, mystery soon gives way to the solid realities of Pictish art and culture, founded on the rich agricultural lowlands of Fife, Perthshire, Angus, Aberdeenshire, Moray, the eastern firths, and Sutherland. Pragmatically, the Picts were wealthy and well organised. Moreover they saw off first the Romans, then the Anglo-Saxons, and the Viking onslaught on Scotland, ceding proportionately far less territory and control to the Norsemen than mainland England or France. They were hardy and well organised when it came to fighting. The Picts were also lovers of the chase as the sculptured stones vividly depict, fond of ornament and colour, and given to tattooing their own bodies with intricate designs so characteristic as to become their distinguishing feature to outsiders.

As for religion, this region is also rich in prehistoric remains, but Christianity was embraced early and expressed through Pictish culture with elaboration and conviction. This laid the foundations of a rich medieval church culture, which in turn became the Presbyterian parish system, though with notable centres of Episcopal resistance. Each period built on the next, leaving an unrivalled sequence of sites and buildings to be explored today. Local culture in its modern Scots form is marked by reserve and understatement – nothing it seems is more Pictish than the Scots, or more Scottish than the Picts.

MORNING

Thanks to you always, O gentle Christ
That you have raised me freely from the black
And from the darkness of last night
To the kindly light of this day.

Thanks be to you, O God, that I have risen today
To the rising of this life itself;
May it be to your glory, O God of every gift,
And to the glory of my own soul.

Thanks in all ages and spheres to you, Holy Spirit
That you have breathed a new day into being;
O Blessed one that seeks my heart, my heart,
Cover me with the shadow of your wing.

BLESSING

Bless to me, O God,
Each thing my eye sees
Each sound my ear hears
Each scent on my nostrils
Each taste to my lips
Each note to my song.

Wisdom of serpent be thine,
Wisdom of raven be thine,
Wisdom of valiant eagle.

Voice of swan be thine,
Voice of honey be thine,
Voice of the Son of the stars.
Bounty of sea be thine,
Bounty of land be thine,
Bounty of the Father of heaven.

Stage 1: Dundee to Glens of Angus
By Meigle, Glamis and Kirriemuir

Dundee is the capital of Tayside, beautifully sited above the widening firth. A flourishing medieval and modern city, Dundee is enjoying a contemporary renaissance. The historic centre has lost much of its older fabric but the medieval Steeple still defines the townscape. Beneath it are a modern evangelical church, cleared of pews, and a more traditional High Church of St Mary, physically joined together. To the west, St Paul's and St Peter's Protestant churches, along with the modest Gothic Revival Roman Catholic Cathedral, add to the steeples. To the east by the Overgate, you reach St Paul's Episcopal Cathedral whose interior has been beautifully restored with its colourful liturgical artwork, and made welcoming to visitors. The art galleries are also excellent in Dundee making it a visual city which glitters in bright weather beside the 'silvery Tay'.

Our journey goes inland by back roads to Camperdown, Liff and Fowlis. Kirkton of Liff is a very old church site, while the medieval kirk of Fowlis Easter shelters the most important pre-reformation church paintings in Scotland, with the strong late-medieval emphasis on the human suffering of Christ. Finding the main road to the north we cross the Sidlaw Hills to Coupar Angus, where one of Scotland's major medieval abbeys once held sway – now a modest ruin. Next we head east to Meigle where the museum houses an unrivalled collection of early carved stones. The most striking thing about these sculptures, apart from their technical artistry, is their combination of Pictish and Christian symbols, whether applied in succession or simultaneously. These stones are unique and unmissable.

Next across Strathmore – the great strath – we reach the attractive village of Alyth where the early church was dedicated to St Moluag – fragments are still to be seen by the present parish church. But interest here also attaches to the Airlie Castle and Kirkton of Airlie a little to the east, north of the main road, where one of Scotland's oldest noble families made its mark in war, ballad and devotion. The church here preserves a notable depiction of the five wounds of Christ. North of all this lies scenic Glen Isla, reaching into the Grampians.

We continue, however, south, winding back across Strathmore to Glamis. In Den of Glamis, St Fergus had a retreat, now marked with a riverside walk, and on the upper bank is Glamis Church and manse with its superb carved cross slab. Glamis Castle, associated with the late Queen Mother and much earlier Macbeth, lies a little to the west. Shakespeare's villain is remembered in Celtic tradition as 'the good King Macbeth' and had no part in the death of Duncan. Our route turns back to the edge of the Grampians and the handsome village of Kirriemuir, birthplace of J.M. Barrie, whose early home can be visited. The parish kirk is on a very old central site, and has attendant chapels in the lovely Glens Clova and Prosen to the north. Those with time should explore at least one glen to experience how this characteristically lowland Scots settlement with its weavers, schools and kirks was actually on the edge of Gaelic speaking highlands. This is the origin of Barrie's imaginative sense of living between two worlds – the practical and the uncanny – which animates all his work.

Stage 2: Kirriemuir to Stonehaven
By Forfar, Aberlemno and Brechin

From Kirriemuir to Forfar is a short hop for anyone but a local, as rivalries were once intense. Forfar is the county town and wears its status openly with some fine architecture, including the churches. The old parish kirk is on its original site in East High Street, while the Lowson Memorial Church is almost a cathedral. However to catch the early atmosphere of Christianity here we need to go a little further east to peaceful Restenneth Priory. Here St Boniface baptised Nechtan King of the Picts close to the site of his epoch-making victory over the Anglo-Saxons to the south at Dunnichen. This was one of the many occasions when, had Nechtan lost the battle, there might never have been a Scotland. Later, St Margaret supported the Celtic Church of Restenneth, and it became in due course a medieval priory.

Turning left beyond the priory we join the Aberlemno road passing the prehistoric fort on Finavon Hill. Here the Picts held powerful sway as is demonstrated by the four Aberlemno stones, three at the roadside and one in the churchyard. If any Pictish superlatives had survived they would be in order now as these stones display the 'mysterious' symbols, hunting scenes, angels and the crosses that are like the full page of an illuminated manuscript.

Next we continue to Brechin which is as perfect a little cathedral town as Britain possesses, with its medieval form largely intact. But before the medieval cathedral Brechin was a Celtic or Culdee monastery as the striking Irish style round tower shows. Here, Pictish patronage and Irish devotion met. The interior displays aspects of all these phases in surviving features and helpful interpretation. Brechin is the pilgrimage centre of Angus and the Mearns and is gradually reawakening to that role. The Cathedral is dedicated to the Holy Trinity.

We go north next, to Edzell, where the castle with its fine renaissance ornamentation and the old church of St Laurence lie west of the modern village at the mouth of Glen Lethnot. Due north of Edzell itself is the more major Glen Esk, last of the Angus Glens, which was a centre of Episcopal loyalties. In consequence, the old chapel in the glen was burned after the 1745 Jacobite Rising, but later rebuilt on lower ground. St Drostan was missionary of the glen, which reaches deep into the Grampians.

Our main route continues to Fettercairn, but again the main action here is a little out of the present attractive village. Going north towards the Cairn O Mount Pass, Dunfothir Hill Fort rises at the west end of Strathfinella. This was an ancient Pictish fortress associated with the Celtic Mormaers or Earls of Angus. Finella, a real-life lady Macbeth, murdered King Kenneth here in revenge for the death of her son. In due course this fortress was moved south-east to Kincardine Castle, of which little now remains, yet it too was a mighty Pictish and, later, royal stronghold, which gave its name to the later county of Kincardineshire. There was a Chapel of St Catherine at the castle.

Geography is critical here as the Howe of the Mearns narrows to the Mounth separating the Mearns from the Aberdeenshire lowlands. The old church of Fordoun, now confusingly in Auchenblae on a wooded ground above the village, was founded by St Ternan of Banchory who brought relics of Palladius, the very early Irish missionary to Scotland, here to kick-start his own Pictish Christian endeavours. A later medieval priest, John of Fordoun, was one of the first historians of Scotland. In the twentieth century, Howe of the Mearns gave birth to Lewis Grassic Gibbon, whose *Scots Quair* captures the history and spirit of the area in some of modern Scotland's finest prose. Our journey continues through the Mearns to the port and holiday town of Stonehaven.

ON THE WAY

SUNSET SONG

Three minister creatures came down to Kinraddie to try for its empty pulpit. The first preached early in March, a pernickety thing as ever you saw, not over five feet in height, or he didn't look more. He wore a brave gown with a purple hood, like a Catholic creature and jerked and pranced round the pulpit like a snipe with the staggers, working himself up right sore about *Latter Day Doubt in the Church of Scotland*. But Kinraddie had never a doubt of *him*, and Chris coming out of the kirk with Will and father heard Chae Strachan say he'd rather sit under a clucking hen that *that* for a minister. The second to try was an old bit man from Banff, shaking and old, and some said he'd be best, he'd have quietened down at his age, not aye on the look for a bigger kirk and a bigger stipend. But the poor old brute from Banff seemed fair sucked dry. He'd spent years in the writing of books and things, the spunk of him had trickled out into his pen, forbye that he read his sermon; and that fair settled his hash to begin with. So hardly a soul paid attention to his reading, except Chris and her father, she thought it fine; for he told of the long dead beats of the Scottish land in the times when jungle flowered its forests across the Howe and a red sun rose on the steaming earth that the feet of man had still to tread; and he pictured the dark, slow tribes that came drifting across the low lands of the northern seas, the great bear watched them come, and they hunted and fished and loved and died, God's children in the morn of time; and he brought the first voyagers sailing the sounding coasts, they brought the heathen idols of the great Stone Rings, the Golden Age was over and past and lust and cruelty trod the world; and he told of the rising of Christ, a pin-prick of the cosmic light far off in Palestine, the light that crept and wavered and did not die, the light that would yet shine as the sun on all the world, not least the dark howes and hills of Scotland.

(from *Sunset Song* by Lewis Grassic Gibbon)

Stage 3: Stonehaven to Arbroath
By Dunnottar and Montrose

Stonehaven grew through a combination of harbours, the original settlement being inland at Fetteresso. But it is a traditional town known for its New Year fire ceremony, when blazing fire balls are swung through the streets. South of the town, on the wild coast of the Mounth, is the spectacular castle of Dunnottar, succeeding a Pictish fortress on the same cliff-top location. Many sieges and battles have taken place at this vital pinch point between north and south, though the siege of royalists here by roundheads in the seventeenth century attracts notice because of the way Scotland's crown and sceptre were smuggled out by the heavily pregnant wife of the minister of nearby Kinneff Kirk. They were hidden for a time under the pulpit there, until Charles II was safely restored. Before reaching Kinneff, we turn down into Catterline Bay, which has been immortalised in the paintings of Joan Eardley – 'the houses are sledging/ down the hill/ in the blind gaze/ of a pandrop moon', as Gerda Stevenson describes it, 'all lights out/ except for one/ its tilted frame/ a well of yellow light/ beacon for travellers'.

After Kinneff comes Inverbervie with its fishing village of Gourdon, but the older Mearns is found more complete a little inland at Arbuthnott. Both Castle and Kirk here are venerable, the latter originally dedicated to Ternan. Also worth a visit is the Lewis Grassic Gibbon Heritage Centre, as no-one has ever written so evocatively of his home turf. Coming back to the coastal road, we pass Johnshaven to reach St Cyrus. The church here has been moved inland due to pressures of the sea, with the fine traditional church above the village, while the original site at Ecclesgreig beneath the cliff by the river mouth retains its atmospheric location and remains.

St Cyrus is a short leg from Montrose, which is a classical town with a rich history and cultural heritage. There is much fine architecture here, and prosperous Montrose played a notable part in the Scottish Reformation through the scholarly and earnest local laird, Erskine of Dun. Again, Montrose was to the fore in the twentieth-century Scottish literary renaissance, with Violet Jacob, Hugh MacDiarmid, Willa and Edwin Muir, Fionn MacColla and George Elder Davie the philosopher, all living here at some point. The Parish Church is on its original site, dedicated in medieval times to St John the Baptist. There was a Celtic monastery on Rossie Island west of the main town in the mouth of the South Esk, also known as Inchbrayock. Two fine cross slabs from this site can be seen in the excellent Montrose Museum.

The coast road runs on through pleasant country to Arbroath, but just before entering the town, turn right to the older site of St Vigeans. Here the Celtic church of St Fechin was founded on an existing sacred mound, and the location is rich in early carvings, now housed in the cottage museum below the church. Local legend has Arthur's adulterous wife Vanora, also known as Guinevere, being executed here, which points up the close connections between the Picts and British Celtic culture. One of the stones in the museum bears the name Drosten, which is cognate with Tristan. Fechin is supposedly buried in nearby Grange of Conon.

Arbroath proper is grouped around its harbour and its abbey, which was founded by King William the Lion in honour of the martyred Thomas Becket and as the place for his own royal burial. Scots kings, it was implied, don't murder archbishops. The Abbey ruins, now complemented by a sensitively designed visitor centre, are impressive, and the latter-day churches crowd round the Abbey site. Arbroath is a bright, beachy place with bracing seaside walks. Hospitalfield House, originally the Abbey hospital, on the south side of town, is a mecca of the visual arts, created by the last eccentric laird of Hospitalfield, Patrick Allan-Fraser. The coast road continues pleasingly by Carnoustie, Monifieth and Broughty Ferry, back to Dundee and the shining Tay.

EVENING

Whoever dwells in the secret place of the
most high
Will be under the shadow of the almighty.
I will say to God, he is my tower and refuge,
I will put my trust in him.
He will set you free from the trapper's snare,
He will cover you with his feathers
And shelter you under his wings
His faithfulness will be your shield and rampart.
You will not fear the terror of night
Or the arrow that flies by daylight
Nor for the plague that walks in darkness
Nor for the wasting fever at midday.
For he shall give his angels charge over you
To keep you in all your ways,

They will carry you up in their hands
And not allow your foot to strike a stone;
You shall walk upon the jackal and the adder
And tread upon the lion and the dragon.
(*from Psalm 91*)

BLESSING

I saw a stranger today
I put food for him in the eating-place
And drink in the drinking-place
And music in the listening-place.
In the Holy Name of the Trinity
He blessed myself and my house,
My goods and my family.
And the lark said in her trill
Often, often, often
Goes Christ in the stranger's guise
O oft and oft and oft
Goes Christ in the stranger's guise.

Route Twelve
The Western Edge:
A Hebridean Saints'
Pilgrim Journey

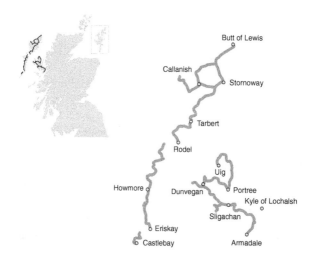

The Outer Hebrides represent one of the far flung frontiers of the Celtic missionary travellers. Seeking 'a place of resurrection', these intrepid and determined individuals were prepared to follow literally the Gospel command to go to the ends of the earth. From here they also pushed on to Caithness, Orkney, Shetlands, the Faroes, Iceland and Greenland. Their means of transport was normally small hide-covered boats that rode buoyantly over the big waves. It must have taken a lot of courage, or faith, or more likely both.

Each part of the Journey has a different character. Skye is mountainous and massive, like an extension of the mainland. It is hard to know sometimes that you are actually on an island. The east and west sides of Skye are very different and the missionary influences are different on each of the interlocking peninsulas that form the island massif.

The Western Isles are undoubtedly islands, and the sea is ever present. Yet there are also significant differences between Lewis and Harris even though they are physically joined. Likewise North and South Uist are very different, with the trend as one travels south being towards a gentler terrain and the even closer sough of the sea. The outer isles, like some coastal areas of Skye, have been well populated since prehistory and contain a wealth of early remains. In some ways prehistory is more present here than the early Christian era with its numerous chapels and beehive cells, many of which have now succumbed to sand and sea. The first wooden churches are long gone.

The instinct to memorialise the landscape continues in the contemporary period, with striking stone monuments commemorating the struggle to regain some share of the land after the clearances of island populations in the nineteenth century, and rural depopulation in the twentieth. At the end of the journey, Barra is the perfect island, like the golden boss of a Celtic shield, set in an emerald sea. Overall, what this Journey reveals is the closeness between the natural world and the older spirituality, which may also be the new spirituality. Keep your eyes open for seals, otters, eagles, dolphins and deer. All of these creatures feature in early Celtic art, not least in the intricately illuminated manuscripts created by the monks.

MORNING

Travelling to the edge,
barrier of the western waves
plains of the Atlantic sea,
islands washed by light,
rinsed by sharp salt water,
we find the viewing points
and look out to far horizons,
wide spaces, outside and within.

BLESSING

Sun Cross, salt wave
Green sea, blue hill
White foam, deep dark,
Let every changing colour
Sing creation's hymn,
Make in your eyes.
The sign of hope
And bridge across
The stormy waters –
Peace haven for your soul.

Stage 1: Armadale to Dunvegan
By Sligachan and Glendale

Skye has over nine hundred miles of coastline, and a series of complex peninsulas or 'wings', giving rise to the name Sgitheach, 'the winged isle'. The early Christian sites are distributed along the two sea channels to the west and east. We begin to the south at Armadale where you can arrive by road or ferry. Isle Ornsay – the island of St Oran – in the Sound of Sleat watches over the southern approaches with its lighthouse and ruined chapel. Proceeding by the eastern side, Pabay or Priests's Isle is off Broadford with its early ruined chapel. Also on the shoreline, south-east of Broadford just before the village of Skulamus, is St Moluag's Well and Baptistery. Turn right at the minor road to Lower Breakish. This important site is at Acaish just beyond the burial ground. The rock on the opposite side of the stream is known as the saint's preaching rock – a missionary outpost of Maelrubha's headquarters at Applecross on the mainland. Next off Loch Ainort is the island of Scalpay, which also has an early chapel, now in ruins, beside Scalpay House. These eastern islands continue with Raasay which looks over to the mainland at Applecross. Access to Raasay is by ferry from Sconser. Close to Raasay House is the Celtic chapel of St Moluag, who is a presence all up the east side of Skye to Kilmaluag at the northern tip. There is a Pictish symbol stone carved in the rock on the shore by the chapel with a cross and the chi/rho symbol of Christ. Raasay is known in modern times as the birthplace of the Gaelic poet, Sorley MacLean, and for the homemade road which Calum MacLeod doggedly created over many years to the north end. North of Raasay is the island of Rona, sometimes called South Rona to distinguish it from North Rona off the Butt of Lewis. This Rona has a ruined chapel, An Teampull, built with rubble and shell lime. On the east of the island is the Giant's Cave, which seems to have been used as a place of early worship. Rona is now uninhabited and can only be reached by hiring a boat, from an experienced local sea-goer able to negotiate its rocky landing places safely.

At Sligachan we swing west up into the Cuillins. This is a dramatic route, celebrated by Sorley MacLean in his epic poem on the mountains. The road leads to Drynoch, birthplace of a much earlier but equally famous poet, Mary MacLeod. From there you can go southwards into Minginish. At Borline on the shores of Loch Eynort is an important early settlement at Kilmoruy. This was the Church of St Maelrubha, founded from his monastery at Applecross on the mainland. The shaft of a Celtic High Cross still stands in the burial ground, depicting the crucifixion on one side and an abbot on the other. This may be an image of Maelrubha. The alternative Minginish road leads to the Talisker Distillery.

Returning north by the same Glen Eynort road, we continue up the coast by Bracadale. Headlands and islands appear to the west where we get our first sightings of Skye's sea cliffs, which are the highest in Britain. On the shore of Loch Caroy there is an Episcopal burial ground, St John's Chapel, where there is a memorial to Flora Swire who was killed in the Lockerbie bombing, Scotland's worst peacetime atrocity.

Before reaching Dunvegan, take the left hand road to Glendale. We are now in Duirinish in the far north-west, with its scattered townships, some of them abandoned in the clearance times, and ancient connections with Ireland. The valley of Glendale, which starts high up at MacLeod's Tables, opens towards the Minch with some fine views over to Uist on a clear day. Glendale was a centre of the Druidic religion, and Columba came here to establish Christianity. An early burial ground lies at the mouth of the glen with a chapel mound. The font survives in a gatepost towards the river. There are also substantial remains of a monastery further up the glen, accessible only by foot. The earliest dedication here was to Congan, an associate of Columba.

Coming back towards Dunvegan, which is the main village in the north-west, we see Dunvegan Castle, the ancient fortress of Clan MacLeod, on the far side of Loch Dunvegan with its strategic, sheltered anchorage. The old Church of St Mary sits above the village and there is an attractive 'Two Churches Walk' taking you along the gentle hillside and then back round to the present Duirinish Parish Church at the north end of Dunvegan.

Stage 2: Dunvegan to Tarbert, Harris
By St Columba's Isle, Portree and Uig

Although St Mary's Church in Dunvegan is an early Celtic Christian site, it may not have been the main church settlement in this area. At Annait, which means 'Mother Church', a mile north of the Fairy Bridge at the foot of the Vaternish peninsula, there was a substantial early settlement, which is worth the short detour from our road to Portree. The monastery was built on a promontory between two deep gullies through which the burns cascade. The cashel, or enclosing wall, is quite distinct, along with the foundations of a chapel and several beehive cells. The site, like many in Skye, has not been excavated and we do not know with which of the early saints it is associated. At Trumpan, near the north end of Vaternish, a ruined church is the site of a notorious clan massacre when Clanranald MacDonalds burnt a MacLeod congregation alive. However, a fierce battle followed, as the MacLeods raced to the scene. The Fairy Flag of Dunvegan was unfurled, and the MacDonalds were driven off with great loss of life.

We do, however, know that the next of our major sites, at Skeabost at the head of Loch Snizort, is named for Columba. St Columba's Isle is formed by two branches of the beautiful tumbling Snizort as it finds its way in to the sea. It is a perfect location with shelter, abundant fish and clean water, as well as excellent sea links. Peace reigns on this green inward isle with its chapels, old carvings, and burial ground. However, in early times this may have been a busy location, and for a time in the mediaeval era it was the centre of the Bishopric of the Isles. Our route swings again south-east to Portree, the capital of Skye. It owes its prominence to a fine natural harbour. On a tidal island in the bay is the ruined chapel of St Columba, while a number of churches lend the town part of its pleasant character.

From Portree we go north to circle the Trotternish peninsula. The coastal views are very fine over to Rona and the mainland, and as we pass the Old Man of Storr on our left, the vistas over to Wester Ross become breath-taking. Kilmaluag is at the north end but there is little evidence of visible remains other than the rocky fragments of Duntulm Castle on the cliffs round the headland. The church here was moved to Kilmuir. The road turns south to Kilmuir where the ruined church and its burial ground are on a slope above the bay. Also here is the Skye Museum of Island Life. South of Kilmuir, on the right hand side of the road, lies Loch Chaluim Cille – St Columba's Loch – now drained. A stony mound marks the former island, and the foundations of the enclosing wall, beehive cells and two chapels can be seen.

Coming down towards Uig, we pass Kingsburgh which is associated with Flora MacDonald, the woman who saved Bonnie Prince Charlie from capture. This is one of the few Gaelic-speaking parts of Skye remaining. Though the area is rich in prehistoric remains the old church is no longer visible, but the present denominations are well represented.

The traditional parish church at Kensalyre has been handsomely restored. Uig is our gateway to the Outer Hebrides, with a car ferry sailing regularly to Tarbert on Harris, which is a fine bracing voyage with island vistas when visibility is good.

ON THE WAY

ARTBRANAN COMES TO COLUMBA

Adomnan's Life of Columba preserves events from Columba's life that were especially valued in the traditions of Iona. There is less about Columba's career in Ireland. Especially striking is a story located specifically in Skye, probably on the island settlement of Skeabost, now known as St Columba's Isle. It seems likely that Artbranan was a Pictish Chief who was honoured in war and for his Druidic faith. All the more significant then that the Columban tradition describes him as 'blameless':

One day, as the saint was staying for a few days in the island of Skye, he struck the seashore with his staff, and said to his attendants, 'Strange, my children, but today a pagan, a venerable man whose conduct has been blameless throughout his life, will receive baptism, die and be buried on this spot.'

Lo and behold, about an hour later, a boat came into the anchorage, and in its prow sat a feeble old man, chief of the Geona. Two young attendants lifted him out of the boat and brought him to the saint.

After being taught by Columba, through an interpreter, the old man believed and was baptised with the flowing water. And when holy communion was administered he died on that spot, in accordance with the saint's prophecy. He was buried there by his companions, who raised a cairn over his grave. A cairn may still be seen there to this day and the river is named for Artbranan.

Tradition assigns this spot to the northern end of St Columba's Isle, and the encounter marks a turning point in Columba's mission, in which he seems to have persuaded many that Christianity was a fulfilment of ancient Druidic belief. 'Christ,' Columba said, 'is my Druid'.

BLESSING

May our search for truth be lifelong,
Without prejudice or rancour.
Let us welcome the good in all,
And deepen our understanding of difference
As the journey continues,
Till coming full circle, we meet
In a place of reconciliation,
Unity and completion, in perfect accord
With the human and the divine.

Stage 3: Tarbert, Harris to Butt of Lewis By Gallan Head and Callanish

From Tarbert we journey north through the lochs and highlands of North Harris. Together Lewis and Harris form the largest island in Britain – collectively known as the Long Island. The sweep of the landscape is on a grand scale, moving from open moorland to mountains in the south and rocky promontories to the west. There is a St Columba's Island to the east at the mouth of Loch Erisort, but in due course we turn west to Achmore, and then divert, before reaching Callanish, onto the long road to Gallan Head. This is remote seaboard country with its own distinctive appeal to the early Christian communities. About a mile short of Gallan Head on the western shore is Taigh a' Bheannaich, the House of Blessing. Further down the coast on the minor road, we reach the site of Taigh nan Caileachan Dubha, the House of the Black Women. This was a Benedictine nunnery in medieval times. Returning by the same road, we pass the turn north to Bernera and Little Bernera where, on Eilean Fir Chrothair, a number of beehive cells survive – the dwellings of remote anchorites in the Celtic period, which are still called locally Am Beannachadh, the Blessing Place. Access to the island is only by special arrangement.

Back on the main road, Callanish is the hinge of western Lewis. It is not one stone henge but a multiple series of ancient monuments creating a sacred landscape on the large scale. Callanish is best viewed as a theatre of land and sky, since it may be the relationship between the distant mountains and the movements of the moon that gives the over-all complex its original purpose. Callanish leads on to a series of interesting locations. The Dun Carloway Broch and the Blachhouse township at Na Gearranan provide essential local context. Many of the early chapels have disappeared below the sand but Teampull Eoin, St John's at Bragar, gives a good sense of the surviving remnants. Further north at Galson, Teampull nan Cṛo Naomh is sited on the machair beyond the farmhouse, open to sea and sky.

Pride of place, however, has to go to the complex of buildings at the north end in the area of Ness. Here, Teampull Moluidh, St Moluag's Church at Eoligarry, was re-roofed in modern times, so preserving an important early church almost complete. The building shows some Norse influence, being at one time dedicated to St Olaf, and is later in date than the original foundation of Moluag. The stone font is from an earlier chapel on the Flannan Isles far to the west. St Moluag's was an important site of pilgrimage and of healing, closely associated with the former St Ronan's Chapel and Well a few hundred yards to the north-east, now a mound of stone. Nonetheless this site points a further sixty miles out to sea where Ronan fled in search of peace. A remarkably whole chapel and cell survive on Rona, while nearby Sulasgeir, and beyond the Flannans and St Kilda, were also 'landfalls of the saints'. The ecologist Frank Fraser Darling stayed on Rona for a time with his family to study the seal colony, leaving a vivid account of life on the edge of the world. Nearer at hand is the Chapel of St Peter on the lovely shoreline of Swainbost.

The Butt of Lewis Lighthouse is as far as we can go by land. One can see why, in early times, this area was the cultic centre of the sea god Shony. Offerings were made to the god on his festival of 1st November, long after the arrival of Christianity, when someone would wade out into the sea to throw specially brewed ale into the waves in the hope that the fertility of the sea would reciprocate with abundant fish and seaweed. Ronan reputedly fled from Ness on a whale in search of some peace, while his sister went to Sulasgeir. Scoured by wind, rain and spray they chose 'prisons of hard stone to bring all to heaven'. As mentioned, the place of resurrection might be at the ends of the earth – and sea.

Stage 4: Butt of Lewis to South Uist By Stornoway and Rodel

The journey now turns back southwards to traverse the whole length of the Outer Hebrides. For scenery, wildlife and the play of light and sky, this route is unique and to be savoured. Stornoway, which is the capital of Lewis, is an untypical urban settlement for this region, with its busy harbour, industries, shops and a cluster of more modern churches. The older church site is the substantial Ui Columba by the sea at Aignish to the east, in the direction of Point, which retains a more traditional island character, albeit nowadays a crofting suburb of the bustling capital.

The road south retraces our route from Harris, but the island is best seen on a circuit, showing how the more fertile west side was given over to larger farms while the people were cleared to the rocky east, where they struggled to make a living from stony soils and the sea. There is an ancient chapel and well in the south-east on the Tore peninsula which was dedicated to St Maelrubha, and was once one of the island's main parish churches. However the Church of St Clement at Rodel dwarfs anything else in the Hebrides as a major piece of late medieval religious architecture. The church was created as a burial place for the MacLeod chiefs, and the carvings on their tombs vividly convey the worldly and spiritual mentality of the Highland aristocracy at this time.

A ferry from Leverburgh takes us on to Berneray and North Uist, where a cluster of early Christian remains exists at the north end. The Teampull Chaluim Cille is in the old burial ground at Clachan Sannda, with the Priest's Stone and St Columba's Well a little further south. This is a very old site. Taigh Chearsabhagh in Lochmaddy is an excellent place to connect with the environment, prehistoric remains and more recent history of the island. Pobull Fhinn stone circle, west of Lochmaddy, shows how the early religious sites and the landscape are so inextricably linked. The most interesting early Christian site surviving in North Uist is Teampull na Trionaid at Carinish in the south-west, which was rebuilt by Bethag, prioress of the nunnery on Iona, and daughter of Somerled, the first Lord of the Isles. Later, it was known as a place of learning served by a traditional order of scholarly priests, the McVicars.

The Carinish stone circle is a little to the east on the road to Benbecula. Across the causeway, the main early locations are on the west side beyond the airfield. Teampull Chaluim Cille is in Balivanich, Monks' Town, on a rise which was once a small island in a now-drained loch. The well is to the south-west, and this supply of fresh water must have been one of the attractions. Carmichael records a tradition that a St Taran came ashore on the sea bay where he wanted to found his Columban settlement, but angels guided him inland to this superior site. South-west on the coast is Nunton, Baille nan Cailleach, where the ruined chapel of St Mary is a successor to an earlier nunnery. The balance of male and female is interesting in these early Celtic foundations.

Stage 5: South Uist to Barra
By Eriskay

Crossing into South Uist, again by causeway, the crofting townships are more on the fertile west side, with hillier ground to the east. It is worth turning right towards Iochdar and Clachan for the lie of the land and sea, though the old chapel ground at Cill Amhlaidh has few visible remains. In general South Uist shows religious continuity with early chapels replaced on the same sites, and then succeeded, often in other locations, by the present Roman Catholic parish churches, all of which merit a visit. Back on the road south, the Catholic identity of South Uist is dramatically marked by Hew Lorimer's monumental lighthouse of a statue – Our Lady of the Isles. Fine views can be had from the statue.

We soon arrive at Howmore, perhaps the most important medieval religious centre in the Western Isles. There were two churches here, St Mary's and St Columba's, and three chapels. Significant remains of four of these survive along with the current Protestant parish church. It is an evocative place in which the grouping of these buildings within a protective cashel remains largely intact. Communication by land and sea was the basis of widespread influences and connections. Howmore is witness to the medieval civilisation of the Western Isles, which was fostered by the Lords of the Isles and in this area by the succeeding MacDonald Clan Chiefs.

South of the ruined clan castle of Ormaclete at Bornish there is a substantial Roman Catholic parish church, which has on older feel than its nineteenth-century date. A walk from here onto the shoreline is an attractive option on a good day. Curious seals investigate close to shore. A little further on, the Museum at Kildonan is an excellent account of local life in past times. Lochboisdale is less interesting than its capital status might suggest, but continuing on the west side is more rewarding with fine outlooks south and out to sea. Kilpheder was the historic parish centre and has a present day Roman Catholic Church of St Peter. Pollachar has a traditional inn at what was originally the ferry crossing to Eriskay, but there is a now a causeway to that intensely beautiful little island. Ferries run to North Barra from Eriskay and also from Lochboisdale to Castlebay, Barra's main harbour.

Above the Eriskay causeway sits St Michael's Church, the work of Father Allan MacDonald and his devoted parishioners. Father Allan was a model latter-day priest, who devoted great love and energy to gathering the traditions and language of Eriskay and South Uist. He is an important figure in that continuing relationship between culture and religion in this region. Eriskay heralds the larger, but equally beautiful, Barra.

The premier pilgrim destination must be Cille Barr, St Barr's Chapel, half a mile north of the airport beach. This is a sheltered and often sunny enclave containing a fine medieval church with remains of a south and north chapel. St Barr is likely to be the same person as Finbarr of Cork, a big player in the Irish church. The weathered carvings, along with evidence of continuing devotion, make this a fitting culmination to the whole journey. Tobar Bharra, a pure flowing well, is east of the burial ground.

There is much else of interest in a circuit of the island including the centrally situated Church of Scotland parish church, and fragments of St Brendan's Chapel on the shoreline at Borve. Castlebay is a culturally lively and attractive location where good music is often to be found in the hotels and pubs. There is a handsome Roman Catholic Church above the little town looking out to the impressive Kismul Castle, stronghold of the MacNeil Chiefs. To the south lie the now largely uninhabited Bishop's Isles each with a distinctive history and evocative chapel sites. Vatersay, however, was the site of an important land raid in 1908, when protesters occupied the island to restore crofting. Eventually, despite fines and imprisonment, they won and Vatersay is now connected by a causeway to Barra. The voyage from Castlebay to Oban is a satisfying conclusion – we have really travelled by land and sea.

EVENING

Look ahead to the north-east
At the mighty sea, home of living creatures,
Dwelling of seals; passionate and fine
It is on the flood tide.

There stands above the brethren
A bright, tall, glossy yew;
The melodious bell sends forth a pure keen note
In St Columba's Church.

Bitter is the wind tonight
It tosses the ocean's white tresses,
I have no fear of Norway's wild raiders
Sailing on the Irish Sea.

BLESSING

Call of the skilful lark
Brings me outside to watch
And see its open beak above
Against the speckled cloudy sky,
I will sing my psalms
For holy bright heaven
As a shielding from harm,
For the purging of my sins.
Blessed be the song.

Route Thirteen
By Northern Coasts:
The St Maelrubha
Pilgrim Journey

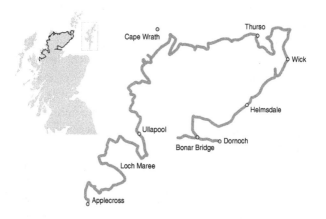

Maelrubha was of mixed Irish and Pictish descent. He came from the area of Derry, a cousin of Columba, but grew up in the monastery at Bangor in north-east Ireland. Just as Columba made Scotland his lifetime's work, so did Maelrubha, dying here after a long busy life. We get the sense of a determined character prepared to take on opposition, if required to achieve his aims. His red hair must have been very distinctive to become his known name – Maelrubha, the red priest.

This story is historically interesting, but becomes compelling because of the geography of Maelrubha's endeavours. Though there are dedications to the red-haired saint in various parts of the Highlands and the north-east lowlands, representing his wide-spread influence, the concentration is in the far north-west, including parts of Skye. This offers the opportunity of a Pilgrim Journey which is, yet again, entirely different from anything yet experienced. This is truly a wilderness journey with long distances, spaced out settlements, and emptiness.

The ambiguous twist however is that some of this emptiness is manmade. There is abundant evidence on all sides of early human occupation and, in the nineteen-twenties, archaeologists uncovered eleven-thousand-year-old Mesolithic remains in four caves on the shores of Loch Assynt. These were hunter-gatherer nomads and their prey included reindeer, bears, lynx and arctic fox. Fuller human settlement waited on the gradual withdrawal of the ice. In the age of the clans there were more people productively existing in the straths, glens and coasts than now. With industrialisation and the concentration of huge tracts of land in a few hands, there was deliberately induced depopulation, clearing people and the cattle on which they depended, sometimes ruthlessly, in favour of sheep and deer for game hunting. The human cost was appalling, and to this day the effects are all too evident.

That said, there are also mountainous sweeps on this route that are a true wilderness. They are formed by very ancient geological processes that make this area one of the oldest natural landscapes, and consequently a geologist's paradise. Here our concern is more with the unique landforms that result. No journey could be more evocative of nature's abstract scale and of the relativity of our human timescales and efforts. For Maelrubha, this was a demonstration of spiritual formation, and a passionate invitation to travel.

To every generalisation, though, there are exceptions and on this route ours is Caithness. Tucked in the north-east corner of the Scottish mainland with a quite different scenic formation from Sutherland, Caithness was a busy and important medieval diocese with an intense layer of kirks and chapels amid the centuries of habitation and building.

MORNING

My heart is steady, O God, my heart is steady,
I will sing and give praise –
Awake, my glory, awake harp and lyre,
I will awaken the dawn
And praise you among the nations
And sing of you among the tribes,
Because your love is like the heavens
And your truth is like clouds in the sky.
Be high, O God, above the heavens
And let your glory cover the earth.
(*from Psalm 57*)

BLESSING

The love and affection of heaven be to you
The love and affection of the saints be to you
The love and affection of the angels be to you
The love and affection of the sun be to you
The love and affection of the moon be to you
Each day and night of your lives
To keep you from haters, to keep you from
harmers
To keep you from oppressors

Stage 1: Applecross to Ullapool

By land this journey has to begin at Lochalsh or perhaps Plockton, which just goes to show that Applecross was a place reached by sea. In compensation we can take the hill road, Bealach nam Bó – Pass of the Cattle – beyond Lochcarron at the head of Loch Kishorn. This rises from sea level to a height of 2,100 feet and then descends again to sea level. The views are spectacular out over Rona and Raasay to the Cuillins of Skye, and to the mainland hills in every direction. This route should not be attempted in snowy or foggy weather.

Applecross itself should be high on the pilgrim destination list. It is a place of peace and beauty, established by Maelrubha as a sanctuary – A' Chomraich. This stretched for six miles and was marked by standing stones inscribed with crosses. In the old burial ground at the beach, the saint himself is at rest. Having died in his labours in Easter Ross, his last wish was to be carried here, but the locals decided he was too prestigious a relic to lose. However, on trying to raise his coffin for burial they found it impossible to lift, until four men came from Applecross, lifted the coffin with ease and bore it back to this final refuge. The grave is traditionally marked by two large stones running east/west, though a standing stone of red granite sent by a princess of Norway in Maelrubha's honour no longer exists. There is a holy well in the trees above, and an old stoup well on the shore. Offshore is the Holy Isle, Eilean na Naomh. The little church, much later than Maelrubha, nonetheless retains the spirit of this special place, so complete despite the passage of centuries.

The route follows Maelrubha north to Shieldaig and Loch Torridon. There is a good landlord story here which is worth recalling as an exception rather than the rule. After one McBarnett had progressively shut down the traditional means of life and livelihood here, Duncan Darroch from Gourock on the Firth of Clyde bought the Torridon estate, and combined deer management with restoration of traditional cattle rearing on the lower slopes of the hills. Everyone thrived in consequence, and when Darroch died in old age at Torridon House, local men carried his body all the way to Gourock for burial. Such is Highland respect. There is a memorial plaque to this event on the road past Torridon, gratefully erected by the widowed Mrs Darroch.

We now follow the River Torridon up towards Loch Maree – Maelrubha's Loch. It is one of Scotland's most beautiful inland lochs. Much of the area is deservedly in the Ben Eighe National Nature Reserve, including the islands. Eilean Ma-Ruibhe is one of the smallest islands but an important place of pilgrimage into recent times. There was a cell or retreat there in the later burial ground; a well of Maelrubha now blocked; and a wishing tree which still stands studded with coins, though it is a lifeless trunk. After the Protestant Reformation, pilgrimage continued here, along with other ancient pagan customs, such as bull sacrifice. Stern efforts were made to suppress these remains of the saint's cult. Access to Isle Maree can only be by special arrangement with the Nature Reserve Wardens. There is an excellent visitor centre at Aultry, a mile west of Kinlochewe, which has all the information on the geology, and the rare flora and fauna, along with latest sightings of peregrine falcons, eagles and pine martens. In the other direction, a short steep drive up Glen Docherty towards Achnasheen gives a spectacular panorama of the loch and surrounding mountains.

Continuing north by the lochside, the road swings west to Gairloch, and then north-east to Poolewe. The beauty of these sea lochs lies not only in their outlook to the west, but in the gentleness of their beaches and lochside settlements where, in contrast to the mountains, people could find shelter and win a living from land and sea. The most famous example of this is the Garden at Inverewe, created by the gardening passion of Osgood Mackenzie who, despite the hard Torridon sandstone, used the equable climate of the lochsides to make a horticultural paradise. Maelrubha established churches in both places, but these have been succeeded by a variety of denominational buildings. If you have time to spend here, minor roads and tracks lead off to the points and headlands, each of which offers fine outlooks seaward to the islands. The beauty then continues north into Gruinard Bay, where the first church at Laide was dedicated to Columba, and then the Loch Brooms.

In historic times this was all a clan battleground between Macleods and Mackenzies. We must negotiate majestic An Teallach high above us before we can pass on to Ullapool, having absorbed the exceptional land and seascape that is Wester Ross – Maelrubha's home parish.

Stage 2: Ullapool to Thurso

Ullapool is a planned fishing village that has grown into a bustling visitor and cultural centre as well. It is also a main port for travel to the Western Isles. The local museums are good, as is the famous Ceilidh Place. The modern churches exhibit a square-set plainness lacking much visible connection with the older spiritual roots. But for our purposes Ullapool is most important as a gateway to Sutherland. At this point in the journey, the landscape begins its turn towards austere wilderness that makes the far north-west so distinctive and unforgettable an experience. For Maelrubha, the intrepid missionary and traveller, this territory presented new challenges and hardships.

There is something surreal and unearthly about the next long stretch to Laxford Bridge. Cul Beag, Stac Pollaidh, Cul Mor, Suilven, Canisp and finally Quinag stand out as if in lonely isolation on a moonscape. In truth they are individual survivors of a once massive mountain range. If time allows it is worth turning west to Polbain, Achiltibuie and the Summer

Isles, so approaching Lochinver on the coast road. You can then stay with the coast on the south side of lovely Eddrachillis Bay, or rejoin the main road directly by Loch Assynt proceeding on the north side of the Bay to Scourie. Another short diversion is possible to Tarbert and the Handa Island bird reserve. This coast is increasingly open towards the North Atlantic, with only the Ness of Lewis visible now directly to the west. It is hard to resist the mystical underlay of this landscape. As the area's most famous modern poet, Norman McCaig puts it, 'Who is it that owns this landscape? The man who possesses it, or I who am possessed by it?'

The direction from Laxford is north-east with possible diversions west to Kinlochbervie, and then further on by special ferry and minibus to Cape Wrath, the nothwesternmost point in the Scottish mainland. It is barren and wild country, but at the Head you may be able to see the Butt of Lewis and the Orkney Islands at the same time. Due north, however, is only the invisible Arctic. The ferry crossing is just short of Durness, and less hardy travellers might head on to there without pause. A little north of Durness is Balnakeil Church and Burial Ground. Founded by Maelrubha in this beachside, yet often windswept, location there has been a succession of historic churches. The eighteenth-century Sutherland poet, Rob Donn Mackay, a Burns of Gaeldom, is buried here. There is also a craft village at Balnakeil, and a little east of Durness are the cavernous, echoing Smoo Caves.

We are now travelling along the top of Scotland by sea lochs and headlands to Tongue, where there is a handsome eighteenth-century parish kirk, traditional burial place of the Mackay Lords of Reay. From Kyle of Tongue look inland to majestic Ben Loyal, while leaving from Tongue itself you can experience the emptiness of the great Sutherland straths by driving south into Strathnaver, and then by Badanloch and Achentoul Forests back to the coast down Strath Halladale. According to one tradition Maelrubha was killed at Skail in Strathnaver by Vikings, rather than dying more peacefully on the Black Isle.

But where did all the people who once lived here go in the Clearance times, and could climate change yet bring people back to these open lands? Back at the coast, Bettyhill is an important clearance township as people were forced to make a living from the sea. But it is also in an area of intense prehistoric settlement. There is a Strathnaver Folk Museum in Farr Old Church, just north of Bettyhill, where the Farr stone is also to be seen with its intricate combination of Pictish and Christian designs. Like Durness, Farr was an important parish centre with little linked chapels scattered out in the sparsely populated area – a very practical way of bringing religion to the people.

Continuing west by lovely Melvich and Portskerra we reach Reay with its historic kirk, and on the east side even older burial ground and chapel site dedicated to St Colm. Colm is a common dedication to a follower or associate of Columba. Next we pass the monumental and ever-controversial Dounreay Nuclear Power Station. No electricity is generated here now but de-commissioning, waste management and the effects of past pollution leave a legacy of many centuries for future generations. Between Dounreay and Thurso, before Bridge of Forss, turn left to reach Crosskirk by the sea. There is a medieval Chapel and Well of St Mary here which shows Norse influence and an old parish kirk. We are firmly arrived in Caithness, a quite different country that looks and feels more like Orkney than Sutherland. The Scrabster Ferry to Orkney is adjacent on this coast.

ON THE WAY

THE BREASTPLATE

We bind unto ourselves today
The virtues of the starlit heaven
The glorious sun's life-giving rays
The whiteness of the moon at even
The flashing of the lightning free
The whirling wind's tempestuous shock
The stable earth, the deep salt sea
Around the old eternal rocks.
Salvation is of Christ the Lord.
We bind unto ourselves today
The strong name of the Trinity.

By invocation of the same,
The Three-in-one, the One-in-three,
Of whom all nature hath creation
Eternal Father, Spirit, Word.
(*Breastplate of St Patrick*)

BLESSING

The keeping of God be upon you in every pass
The shielding of Christ be upon you in every
path
The bathing of Spirit be upon you in every
stream
In every land and sea by which you go
And the keeping of the everlasting father
Upon his own illumined altar.

Stage 3: Thurso to Helmsdale
By Wick and Dunbeath

If time allows it is good to sample inland Caithness
first, rather than simply follow the rocky and dramatic coastline. It is big open country with much
fertile ground rising gradually to moorland and then
hills in the south. The early importance of Thurso
is shown in the substantial ruins of Old St Peter's
Church on the Bay. The Bishop also had a residence
here. But Halkirk, south of Thurso, was the original centre of the Caithness diocese, with dedications

to St Drostan and St Fergus on the site of the old parish church. The more recent planned village here was created by Sir John Sinclair, the agricultural improver.

Rich agricultural land continues on the road to Watten where there was a medieval convent of St Catherine. Coming round the foot of Loch Watten turn back towards Halcro and then Bower, both traditional church locations though the latter is an ivy covered ruin. Going back north towards Castletown divert west to Old Olrig where St Trothan's Church is a fine example of the medieval church sites. Trothan may be a version of St Drostan who is also recalled after the Norse period as St Trostan. There is sense of long tradition here, made somehow more orderly by the period of Norse rule and the subsequent systematic absorption of Caithness into Scotland.

Starting on the coast road there is a more vivid dramatic feel to both the landscape and the history. Some remarkable forts and castles perch on the sea cliffs, but the traditional churches keep coming. At Dunnet the old church is still in use, likewise that at Canisbay, which was dedicated in the founding Celtic period to St Drostan. These locations relate respectively to Dunnet Head and John O Groats, which looks out towards the island of Stroma. Heading south by Freswick and Keiss we approach the exceptional cliff top strongholds of Ackergill, Girnigoe and Castle Sinclair, which speak volumes about the centuries of warlike struggle for power in Caithness. The old county town of Wick comes next with its successive harbour developments and its long importance as a fishing port. The parish church in the High Street was the site of St Fergus' Kirk, and there is a Sinclair burial aisle in the burial ground and a medieval effigy supposedly representing Fergus. Wick has some handsome architecture, including its churches and the Pulteneytown harbour, which was reconstructed by Thomas Telford.

South of Wick there is another grim tower on the cliff as a warning signal that the drama continues, though the road runs inland for a while, returning to the coast at Ulbster. There was a medieval Chapel of St Martin in the burial ground here, now another Sinclair burial aisle. The Ulbster Stack is in the sea a little to the north. Nature's rock artistry is notable in Caithness, inspiring many human imitators. At Whaligoe, further south, access to the harbour is by three hundred steps cut in the cliffs. Three miles south at Clyth is the 'Hill of Many Stanes', a prehistoric construction of over two hundred flagstone boulders in twenty-two rows. Next, north of the main road at Lybster, are the Grey Cairns of Camster, a truly monumental testimony to our ancestors' respect for the dead – and a mighty work in Caithness stone. Lybster is a planned fishing village like Latheronwheel, while Latheron is an older parish centre. The huge burial ground here contains the historic parish kirk, now the Clan Gunn heritage centre, parts of the medieval church absorbed into a burial aisle, and an impressive freestanding bell tower.

We are now approaching the Caithness–Sutherland border once again, but not before stopping at Dunbeath with its magnificent cliff-top castle and a fine heritage centre in the former village school. In trying to tell the story of this part, the centre is in effect telling the story of Caithness. An additional attraction is the focus on the modern novelist and essayist, Neil Gunn, whose work is a saga of Highland history and life that then flows into a spiritual stream. Gunn belongs to Caithness and Sutherland, but his art is universal and a wonderful way to connect with the inner meanings of the landscapes and centuries through which we have travelled.

Stage 4: Helmsdale to Dornoch
By Lairg and Ardgay

As if to demonstrate that we have truly passed out of Caithness back into Sutherland, Helmsdale commands our route and points us towards another of the great straths. The Timespan exhibition in Helmsdale by the Telford Bridge is an excellent interpretative resource, but it is well worth going up at least part of the Strath, which would lead eventually into Strath Halladale, and then returning by the same road. There is a fine clearance memorial in Helmsdale, of a family looking out to sea, which jars somewhat with the gigantic statue of the

Duke of Sutherland, the great clearer, on the hill-side above Golspie. The close connection between the landowners and the ministers of the Church of Scotland led to great disillusion in these parts with the 'Auld Kirk' and to a profusion of dissenting and free churches, as evident in Helmsdale. This was another way, along with the land leagues and direct action such as land raids, in which the crofters gradually fought back against the unrestrained despotic power of wealth. In doing so they appealed to the ancient Celtic belief that 'The earth is the Lord's and all the fullness thereof' – the gifts of creation were for everyone, and not to be dispensed in the private interests of a few, which made even poaching something of a religious duty.

Proceeding by Brora, with its now unworked coal reserves and a modern Roman Catholic Church of Christ the King, we reach Dunrobin Castle, headquarters of the Sutherlands, who are still one of the largest landowners in Britain. The museum here has many historical treasures from all over Sutherland that are well worth seeing, not least the carved stones, though the castle itself is somewhat overblown and over-decorated. Next is Golspie, an attractive village and visitor centre, with the aforementioned statue of the Duke above. Beyond Golspie turn right into Strath Fleet for Lairg to sample some of the area we neglected by keeping far to the west coast on the road north. Maelrubha set up an early church at Lairg of which nothing survives. From Lairg, roads fan out – north to

Altnaharra, north-west by Loch Shin to Laxford Bridge, and west into Strath Oykel. We go south to Bonar Bridge.

The bridge is over the Dornoch Firth but the village is on the east side. This is another area saturated with prehistoric remains. A fine parish church is on the hillside above at Creich, with an older church site and burial ground nearby. The early dedication here was to St Devenick. Across the firth at Ardgay are more traditional Highland churches, some now in disuse. But our route goes north-west into Strathcarron all the way up to Croick. Here, in 1845, the people of nearby Glen Calvie were huddling for shelter, having been cleared from their homes in favour of sheep. About eighty people of all ages were huddled underneath a temporary shelter, considering it irreverent to shelter in the church itself. However some scratched their names and messages on the east window: 'Glen Calvie is a wilderness under sheep . . . Glen Calvie people was in the churchyard here . . . Glen Calvie people the wicked generation . . . resided in the churchyard May 24th 1845.' From embers such as these, the struggle for public ownership of Scotland's land was reignited and continues to burn.

Returning down Strathcarron there are roads north and south of the river. Cross back at Bonar Bridge to proceed east by Skibo to Dornoch. Everything here owes its origins to first the Celtic Chapel of St Barr at the east end of the churchyard, and then the medieval Cathedral. The town was originally the clustered manses of the cathedral clergy and the Bishop's modest Palace, now a hotel. Despite various vicissitudes the present day cathedral retains intact much of its original design and scale; by cathedral standards it is small and perfectly formed. This reflects its purpose as a fitting headquarters for the Diocese of Caithness – which included most of Sutherland. From here the good Bishops could keep in touch by land and sea with their far-flung churches, while also being able to travel south to the power centres of the Scottish kingdom. That said, this was no ecclesiastical sinecure, with bishops often caught in the crossfire of inter-clan and aristocratic rivalries. One was roasted alive. Modern times have been kinder to the cathedral, which possesses some fine modern windows and other ornament.

Dornoch also enjoys a superb coastal location, with easy access to Tain and Portmahomack at the northern end of St Columba's Pilgrim Journey. They are also well worth a visit if not already reached. Altogether, this is a sunny sea-girt place to end the northern coastal pilgrimage, back amid the landfalls of Columba, Barr, Maelrubha, Moluag and the rest.

EVENING

In remote places we slow to the rhythms
Of land and sea, of tides and seasons.

Like Maelrubha we have struggled with the
elements
Like Finbarr we have found places of refuge by
the sands
Like Columba we pause and take stock,
breathing quiet air.
We rest now a while to tell a story or sing a song –
for tomorrow the road will carry us on.

BLESSING

I will bathe my face
In the nine rays of the sun,
As Mary washed her Son
In the blessed milk.
May mildness be on my lips,
May kindness be on my face,
May discipline be on my desire,
May wisdom be in my purpose.
The love that Mary gave to her Son
May all the world give me;
The love that Jesus gave to John Baptist
Grant that I may give to whoever meets me.
May the Son of God make clear my way.
And be at the end of my seeking.

Route Fourteen
On the Sea Roads:
The St Magnus
Pilgrim Journey

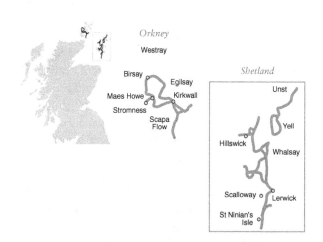

Orkney

Westray

Birsay

Maes Howe

Stromness

Egilsay

Kirkwall

Scapa
Flow

Shetland

Unst

Hillswick

Yell

Whalsay

Scalloway

Lerwick

St Ninian's
Isle

Orkney and Shetland are very different. They are often put together because they are island group-ings north of mainland Scotland, and both wedged between the North Sea and the Atlantic. They have been part of the Norse world as well as the Scottish for centuries, and they share the same patron saint, St Magnus. However the geology, geography and ecol-ogy differ widely. Shetland is above all a place of the sea – a kind of extended harbour – while Orkney, albeit surrounded by sea, is focussed on its rich, well-tilled land. Shetland is predominantly rocky, though with fertile, carefully tended crofts where exposure and climate allow. Orkney, like Caithness, is made of sandstone, which gives its buildings their monumental feel, but most of the ground is gently rolling, and only Hoy and Rousay are predominantly hilly or rocky.

Consequently we will treat Orkney and Shetland differently, journeying through different landscapes and experiences. Nonetheless, both island groupings offer three powerful persuasions to pilgrimage – centuries of evolving religious heritage, a vivid sense of the natural elements, and compact journeys. In addition they have both inspired great art – music, literature, painting and film. Their story begins long before St Magnus, though from the moment of his death on Egilsay his influence has been all pervasive.

The life of Magnus also reminds us that Orkney and Shetland are integral to wider northern seaways. Norway, Sweden, Denmark, the Faroes, Iceland, Greenland and Newfoundland are all in the flow. These also became the sea roads for Christianity.

One of the first Norse rulers to adopt Christianity was Queen Aud, the 'deep-minded', who set sail from Caithness and then Orkney after her son Thorstein's death in Scotland. Aud finally settled in Iceland at Hvamm, building a church at Krossholar, 'for she had been baptised and held strongly to the Christian faith'. When it eventually came, the marriage between Norse culture and the new faith was a fruitful and creative one, as Orkney and Shetland show.

MORNING

Be a smooth way before me,
Be a guiding star above me,
Be a keen eye behind me,
This day, this night, for ever.
I am weary and forlorn,
Lead me to the land of the angels,
Since it is time I went for a space,
To the court of Christ, the peace of heaven.

BLESSING

Be, O God, at peace with me,
Be my support, my helm, my star,
From my lying down
To my rising anew to voyage.

Stage 1: Orkney Rings

Resist the temptation to begin with St Magnus Cathedral in Orkney, as it belongs to a sequence and a story. Instead, take the first ring west along the coast to Orphir. The apse survives here of a famous round church based on the holy sepulchre in Jerusalem, recalling Earl Rognvald's pilgrimage after the building of his cathedral. Continue on the coast road to Stromness, Orkney's second port, which is celebrated as Hamnavoe in the stories and poems of its best-known literary son, George Mackay Brown, whose bench sits on Brinkie Brae above the harbour, still watching all of life go by. Continue north from Stromness on the east side of Loch of Stenness, turning round the head of the loch to view a Neolithic sacred landscape writ large.

It is only in recent years, with the excavation, on Ness of Brodgar, of an enormous Neolithic temple enclosure, that people have realised that this whole area has a unity of design. On this side of the Ness are the Stones of Stenness, and on the other the Ring of Brodgar, and the Ring of Bookan a little to the north-west, as well as, to the south-east, Maes Howe chambered cairn down whose passage the midwinter sunset gleams. The openness of the landscape to sea and sky makes the perfect setting for such cosmic theatre. Awesome, for once, may be the correct adjective.

Returning back over the Ness, we continue north to Skaill Bay where the Neolithic village of Skara Brae is still battling the encroaching sea. Here is the domestic counterpart of the cosmic grandeur. Proceeding north we come to Brough of Birsay which plays an important part in the Magnus story. Here on the tidal island there was a Celtic monastery, later succeeded by a medieval church and Norse settlement. At the mainland village, the church was for a while the bishop's own kirk and it was here that Magnus's remains were brought to be buried, and here that the first miraculous happenings started the Magnus cult against the wishes of both Earl and Bishop.

Follow this story round the north end and down the east side where Rousay dominates the outlook. In the narrows is Eynhallow – the Holy Isle – where there was a medieval monastery. This island often disappears and magically reappears in Orkney folklore. Next appears the island of Wyre, nurse of two famous poets: Bishop Bjarni in the days of the Norse Earls and, in the twentieth century, Edwin Muir, one of the outstanding spiritual voices of his time. North-east of Wyre is Egilsay with the Church of St Magnus on its southern tip. This is where Magnus was murdered on the shoreline – a monument in the meadow marks the spot. The ferry from Tingwall plies to Rousay, Wye and Egilsay.

Swing south to Finstown at the head of Firth Bay, and then we are set fair for our pilgrimage to the great shrine of Magnus at Kirkwall. Here the saint

was enshrined after the move from Birsay insti-
gated by Earl Rognvald and his father Kol, who
may have been the visionary behind the whole proj-
ect. Remarkably for Scotland, the axe-cloven skull
of Magnus remains in position inside the massive
right-hand pillar beside the choir, while Rognvald's
skull is in the left-hand pillar, indicating his later
status as a second saint. This extraordinary survival
receives only a modest mention on a small plaque,
since, as Murdoch Mackenzie observed (approv-
ingly) of Orkney in the eighteenth century, 'the
Religion is Presbyterian, as Established in Scotland,
without Bigotry, Enthusiasm, or Zeal'.

A second ring goes east from Kirkwall to the
Brough of Deerness. This was the site of a substantial early Celtic monastery with chapel and cells,
though access is now difficult because of erosion of
the land bridge. Come back south-east to St Mary's
and then Lamb Holm where the lovely Italian
Chapel was built, and later lovingly restored, by
prisoners of war who never forgot their hospitable
treatment at the hands of the local people. Going on
into Burray and South Ronaldsay, by the Churchill
Barriers built belatedly to protect the Scapa Flow
anchorage from submarine attack, we must imagine
a network of Norse chapels succeeding and extend-
ing the Celtic pattern across the landholdings. Only
some of these survived to become later chapels and
churches, but they demonstrate the ready welcome
that Christianity received in Orkney. At the southern
end of South Ronaldsay, St Mary's Church is one

such site, while at nearby Isbister is the intriguing 'Tomb of the Eagles', a prehistoric burial cairn with its own special symbolism.

If time allows, each of the northern islands has its own sites and attractions, not least Westray and Papa Westray, where there is a very old pilgrimage tradition associated with St Boniface and St Triduana (Treadwell Loch) the healer, which probably predates the Magnus developments.

ON THE WAY

AN EASTER SACRIFICE

The meeting to seal the peace and goodwill between the two earls was to take place on Egilsay, in spring, during Holy Week. Earl Magnus had two ships with the agreed number of men, and set off for Egilsay. But Earl Hakon gathered a large force of fighting men, and as many ships as if he were going to war. Magnus only prayed devoutly at the chapel, and had a mass said for himself. In the morning Hakon and his men hurried ashore.

The illustrious Earl Magnus was as cheerful as if he had been invited to a feast. He spoke neither words of anger nor resentment, but knelt down to pray, covering his face with his hands. Hakon told his standard bearer Ofeig to do the killing, but he angrily refused. So he ordered his cook Lifolf to kill Magnus, but the cook burst into tears.

'There is nothing to weep over', said Magnus, 'an act like this can only bring fame to the man who carries it through. Show yourself a man of spirit and you will have my clothes, according to the old customs. Don't be afraid, you're doing this against your will and he who gives the order carries greater blame than you.'

The Earl Magnus took off his tunic and gave it to Lifolf. Then he stretched himself on the ground, committing his soul to God, and offering himself as a sacrifice. He prayed for himself and his friends, and for his enemies and murderers. He confessed his sins and asked that his soul might be washed clean by the spilling of his own blood. He asked that he might be greeted by God's angels and carried by them into the peace of Paradise. As this friend of God was led to his execution, he said to Lifolf, 'Stand in front of me and strike me hard on the head. It's not fitting for a nobleman to be beheaded like a thief. Take heart, poor man, I've prayed that God grant you his mercy.'

With that, Earl Magnus crossed himself and bowed to receive the blow. So his soul passed away to Heaven.

(*The Orkneyinga Saga*)

BLESSING

Comfort the sorrowful,
strengthen the weak, gently upholding,
deliver the vulnerable and frail from death
so that we may not be exiles
from the kingdom of the living.
(*Aberdeen Breviary, adapted*)

Shetland Slipways

There in Shetland seems a stone's throw from sea. The Norse character seems even more pronounced than in Orkney, in the scenery, the seamanship, and the language with its unique admixture of Scots and Norn. There are more cliffs and more colour, or at least all of these things are more tightly packed than in Orkney. Early Celtic Christianity is surely less significant here? But that is a misunderstanding. Shetland fits perfectly the desirable destination at the ends of the earth. Moreover its rocky cliffs, peninsulas and offshore islands are a wilderness or 'desert' in the Celtic sense of the term – isolated places of retreat and spiritual contemplation. Early Norse chronicles recorded that Shetland was occupied by Picts and Papils, a Celtic culture similar to that of the northern Scottish mainland and the Celtic monks. Many of their early settlements have been literally consumed by the elements, yet archaeologists keep finding more.

The Shetland Museum in Lerwick is a good place to start, sampling the rich succession of cultures and the abundant archaeological record. From Lerwick we go south-west to the old island capital at Scalloway, which, in its turn, had replaced Tingwall as the meeting place of the Shetland Althing, or parliament. The notorious Earl Patrick Stewart built himself a fine castle here after the Scottish takeover of Shetland. It is worth crossing here to Hamnavoe on West Burra.

There was a Celtic monastery on this southern land-fall at Papil and two fine carved stones survive, one still on site. The importance of the monastery, which had a round tower, is also shown by the Monks' Stone in the Shetland Museum. It depicts five monks moving towards a High Cross. Four are on foot, with their leader on a pony, and each one carries a crook and a book satchel for their Gospel manuscript. No artwork in the Celtic world brings us closer to these early missionaries and travellers. The stone is the side panel of a shrine that clearly contained relics of an important individual whose identity has been lost.

From Scalloway we return to the main road south, touching on harbours and brochs. Offshore to the north-east is Bressay which has a church and carved stones, and due east lies Mousa with its outstanding broch, which is a skilfully designed combination of watchtower and prestigious stone dwelling. Back on the west side near Levenwick, a narrow isthmus joins the mainland peninsula to St Ninian's Isle. This was the site of a clifftop Celtic monastery beneath whose chapel the St Ninian's Isle silver hoard was concealed, perhaps in anticipation of a Viking raid. Fragments of a saint's shrine were also excavated here and are on display in Lerwick, though the treasure itself is in the National Museum in Edinburgh. At the foot of the peninsula, definitely unmoveable to Edinburgh, is Jarlshof, an astonishing sequence of settlements built one on top of the other.

Our second loop goes north-west from Lerwick out to Walls and Sandness. There is some fertile

croftland in this region and many inland lochs. South
of the Walls road is the Neolithic settlement and temple of Stanydale. At the end of the road west is Papa
Stour, the priests' island, once a flourishing community and now almost deserted. We must return as we
came in order to go north again, traversing mainland
segments that feel like islands. Muckle Roe, an actual
island, sits solidly to the west.

Keeping north we swing west to Hillswick where
there is an enterprising wildlife sanctuary and cultural centre. Further west is Esha Ness with its cluster of scenic features including the old burial ground
and church site at Crosskirk. Again we must retrace
our steps to go further north to North Roe, arriving
finally at Isbister. Nearby on the east coast at Kame
of Isbister, looking east to Yell, was a major Celtic
monastery in the jaws of the ocean. Archaeologists
have traced nineteen cells or chapels here, with others lost to the waves. It should be stressed that access
to this site is difficult, and that in rough weather
these wild coastlines are hazardous.

Returning south we then go on the north-eastern side to Yell and Unst. These islands have experienced significant depopulation in modern times.
There is, though, plentiful evidence of earlier settlement with chapels at Cullivoe, Kirk of Ness, and
at Mid Yell. At Papil Ness, further north, there is
an even more remote chapel site only accessible by
foot. There was also a large monastery at Birrier,
now completely inaccessible because of the collapse
of the land bridge. St Colman's Episcopal Church

at Burravoe in South Yell, however, shows that not every church is closed or washed into the sea. On Unst there are remains of traditional chapels at Clibberswick by Haroldswick, and to the south at Gletna in Uyea Sound and on Uyea Island. Fetlar, east of Yell, has always attracted those with an eremitic disposition, and there have been modern monastic ventures connected with both Orthodox and Roman Catholic traditions. The main Celtic monastery was on the inaccessible rock stack at Outer Brough – ascetic with a capital 'A'.

We return to Lerwick on the east side where the fishing island of Whalsay is visible offshore. Hugh MacDiarmid, the twentieth-century poet, lived here for a time and wrote some gritty poems in praise of the Shetland fishermen and women. The mainland coast is again multiply indented and rocky. Back in Lerwick, the Magnus story can be found depicted in stained glass in the handsome town hall and again in St Magnus Episcopal Church, which exhibits all the colour of the nineteenth-century liturgical revival. This was a period when Shetland protestants were much influenced by Methodism. The predominant trait is now undoubtedly agnostic or indifferent to institutional religion, but that conceals a keen sense of the natural world, of community values and of an unspoken sense of wider spiritual context. Human life here calls for solidarity in the face of elemental powers of creation and destruction.

EVENING

Broken is the dripping honeycomb
Releasing the sweetness of honey
Dispensing goodness with its fragrant scent.
The holy man is slain
But his miracles arouse wonder
Enlighten the blind, purging anger.
Captives are freed by the martyr's help
And the shipwrecked loosed from death.
Joy comes to the sorrowful, healing to the sick,
And sound hope in time of danger and distress.
The alabaster jar is broken, but the aroma
Spreads far and wide, fragrant anointing.
(*Aberdeen Breviary, adapted*)

BLESSING

O God, who does not let time pass
Without the comfort of the saints,
Grant us we pray this night,
Protection through the gracious intervention
Of your most holy gentle martyr Magnus,
light of the north and star of the sea,
Now and for evermore.
(*Aberdeen Breviary, adapted*)

EVENING ON A LAST DAY

O wisdom of God, sweetly ordering all things,
Flowing from the glory of the eternal,
Making all things new, kind to all,
Making friends to God in all,
The light of life send upon us,
The joy of peace send upon us,
The gladness of goodwill send upon us.
Come at evening time with light
And in the morning with your glory
To guide our feet into the way of peace.

BLESSING

May the wisdom of God guide you,
May the strength of God uphold you,
May the peace of God possess you,
May the love of God enfold you,
Now and to the end of days.
(*Ascribed to St Columba*)

CPSIA information can be obtained
at www.ICGtesting.com
Printed in the USA
BVHW050031231222
654880BV00005B/22